From Being Perfect to Being Real

Cupcakes and Cocaine

Brienne Joelle

iUniverse, Inc.
Bloomington

iUniverse books may be ordered through booksellers or by contacting:

iUniverse
1663 Liberty Drive
Bloomington, IN 47403
www.iuniverse.com
1-800-Authors (1-800-288-4677)

ISBN: 978-1-4502-8623-7 (sc)
ISBN: 978-1-4502-8624-4 (hc)
ISBN: 978-1-4502-8625-1 (ebook)

Library of Congress Control Number: 2011900966

Printed in the United States of America

iUniverse rev. date: 01/14/2011

For my "HunnieBunnies," Conner and Anna—the two of you are the one clear reason I continue to find my way around in this life.

I want to be your clear guide and the light when your own light is dim. Most important, I want to be your companion from here until there is no more. We chose one another for a reason, and I dream that we choose each other again the next time around the block.

To become a champion, fight one more round.

—James "Gentleman Jim" Corbett

Contents

Acknowledgments

I have so many people to thank and recognize who have made this opportunity happen. First and foremost, I want to thank my family—every one of you.

Dad and Mom, you have continued to stand by me and back me up when I have been leaning or falling over. As you have witnessed, when I fall, I really go back end over teakettle. You have given me a lifetime of support, guidance, and advice, and you have also been my best cheering section. I cannot express how much love and gratitude I have for you both.

Next, I have to thank my brother, Chad, and his wife, Kristen. I am forever grateful to you both for your late-night rescues—closing up of bars, too many parties to count, and the rest of my incessant nonsense. I am indebted to you both for never once judging me, always having an open door, and, most of all, having the stamina to deal with me as a family member.

There have been so many friends, coworkers, neighbors, and strangers who constantly helped and supported me along the way. My hope is that you continue to be as open, loving, nonjudgmental, and supportive as you have unknowingly always been.

All the professional people in my life have been the core of guidance that helped me find my way out of darkness. Teachers, doctors, and counselors are never appreciated enough. They are the angels walking the earth among us.

Dani Hart, MS, of Sound Mind and Body ushered in the emergence of my inner artist, writer, mother, caretaker, and confident woman. Your help in finding, nurturing, and valuing my true identity has been beyond valuable. Simply said, you launched me.

Alisa Sylling of Awake in Joy is nothing short of a miracle worker. You healed, supported, and encouraged my awakening. Indeed, you changed my life forever, and I'm thankful for your love and willingness to share your knowledge of endless possibilities. Your lessons, guidance, and teaching forced the goddess within me to stand tall and proclaim: "Yes! I find strength in being fabulous."

For my counselor, Sean Johnson, I want you to know that you greatly annoyed me throughout my treatment. You successfully tackled the job that allowed me to let down my guard in order to open up and talk. I am grateful for that, because you initiated the beginning of my journey. My hat's off to you for willingly listening and enduring copious amounts of craziness as a counselor.

Kathryn Jones, you are my long-lost soul friend. It was nice to have you as a guide and friend to enter this journey with together. You have always been supportive, encouraging, open, and accepting. Thank you for always having a shoulder available to cry on, as well as for being a friend in a parallel universe.

To Sherry Folb, my editor, who has not only guided my writing but also supported and guided my intuitive path without hesitation. You allowed me to feel comfortable exposing and exploring my innermost thoughts and emotions. There is nothing that could shock you, and you have truly given me freedom by never hesitating to hear my words.

For my friend named Fig, thank you for not ditching this *amiga*, and thank you for having the clarity to never judge and abandon. Here is to another twenty years and lifetimes together as friends.

In my friend Asenath Johnston, I have met my match. You rival my humor, can still laugh when knocked down, and can understand what it's like to raise twins. From day one, I've felt that, no matter what, I could tell you anything. We will continue to stand by each other and make it down this road called life. When all else fails, we can always find wisdom at the Poodle Dog, even with a one-mulligan allowance.

And to my ex-husband, you deserve many thanks as well. What can I say? You've been one hell of a soldier.

A sincere shout-out to all of those who never believed in me, doubted my focus, or gossiped about my failures—I did make it.

Preface

Over the past year, I have experienced what would be the equivalent of gold medaling in the Emotional Olympics. That is not an exaggeration. My intention in writing this book is not just to tell my own story but also to inspire others to be open to endless possibilities. It can be difficult to share our personal experiences, but it is important—especially when we feel that by sharing we can help others see that they are not alone. At times I felt alone, ashamed, and embarrassed; frequently, I also felt like I was going certifiably nuts. In part, I wrote this book so that everyone who reads it will know that he or she is never alone.

At the point when I felt most alone, most ashamed, and most afraid, something amazing happened. I took a leap of faith in order to return my life to exactly where I had always dreamed it would go. Now, be aware that what I call a "leap of faith" others might call an "insane jump into the unknown." Then again, that is exactly what a leap of faith really is—jumping across a chasm with nothing to catch you . . . nothing but knowing in your heart and soul that whatever higher power you believe in *will* catch you.

What I offer is a no-nonsense book that confirms what many people already knew—it seemed that everyone knew it *except* me—that I am strong and resilient and worthy . . . that we all make mistakes, and that the only way to set ourselves free of their burden is to forgive ourselves, seek the forgiveness of those we hurt, and move on—one step at a time.

This was not easy to live, write, or recount. I can only hope you find some sliver of wisdom within these pages to use as a tool in order to discover your own individual path. There is no such thing as a how-to for living, but I envision this book as being a kind of how-it-is for living—something that will support, inspire, and comfort all who read it.

Of course, names, dates, and locations have been altered, because I really don't want people knocking on my door and screaming at me for throwing them under the bus. Most of us, at one time or another, have been involved in something we regret or are ashamed of. We are human, so we cannot be perfect; we each can be only who we are, and that is what it means to be real.

1

Start of the Race

One Foot in Front of the Other

Some call life the "grand illusion." I wouldn't say I agree with that description, but life can become an illusion. By that I mean, if we are not careful, what we imagine is important can become more important—more real to us—than what is real. And make no mistake: What is real is what matters—all that matters. If what is real no longer matters to you, it's time to make some significant changes in your life. Using things to make what you feel you can't change more acceptable to you is never an answer. It's an excuse. A way out. A cop-out.

Sometimes, the only way out is the way through; no matter how much or how hard you try to convince yourself otherwise, anything else is an escape. And escaping is just an excuse. When you go through, instead of going around or hiding, you cannot escape or make excuses. The only way through is by living—every day, putting one foot in front of the other, no matter how hard it might be.

Just as we each find a different way out or around, we each find a different way through, a different way to put one foot in front of the other. This morning I was hypnotized; tomorrow I am meeting a group of psychics at a truck-stop diner; currently I sit here debating whether I should meditate.

Who is *this woman?* you may be asking yourself.

There is no quick answer to that question, for me or anyone else. But you're reading this book, and I wrote it, so I'll try to give you a quick, simple answer. Know that the book itself is the complete answer, and I hope you'll read it cover to cover not only in order to find out my answer to who I am, but also as a step toward discovering your own answer to who you are. That answer is all that matters—for any of us.

For the quick answer I promised, here goes. Yes, I am a completely normal person who has not gone over the edge. I have not plunged into the New Age by means of yoga, mystical crystals, or anything else. Believe me: I never thought I would find spirituality in the same place where I had to pee in a cup. (Hmmm—more about *that* later.) I am a woman who got so caught up in the whirlwind that life can be today that I lost my bearings—lost my way—and turned to something I thought would be the answer to my struggle, but that never can be the answer to anyone's struggle: cocaine.

That was the quick answer. Before you read further to find the complete answer (remember, I said the complete answer was the whole book), I know that the quick answer needs a bit of an expansion. Let me back up for a minute so I can explain to you just how bad things were for me when I was a cupcakes-and-cocaine mommy—and some of the reasons why I got to that point in the first place.

The first important thing to understand is that, even though things were out of control, I was somehow able to keep everything together, at least outwardly. On the inside, I was falling apart—feeling the person I was shatter into a million pieces that swirled around me, as life spun increasingly into a tailspin. Yet, on the outside, everything "looked" fine; to onlookers, even people who really "knew" me, I projected a good outer appearance. A fabulous one, in fact, if I may say so. My country-club family—handsome husband, attractive wife (again, if I may say so), and beautiful boy-and-girl twins—seemed perfect. What I realize now is that I never should have taken the precious gift of family for granted; but I did, and I have to live with that.

This book is not a self-pity party; it is not a classic, formulaic fairytale of a girl who had it all—family, money, great shoes, and everything she ever wanted. This is also not a story of a girl who had everything but was still not happy—boo-hoo for poor little Holly Homemaker. This book is not any of those things. Instead, it is a real-life story of a girl who *did* have it all but who felt like she couldn't handle what it took to keep it all—the incredibly hard work and constant stress of maintaining the "perfect" family, combined with the never-ending anxiety of keeping up with all the "perfect" supermoms around her—while struggling to appear fabulous on the outside. When I said I had lost my way, I meant I had lost sight of who I really was and what really mattered; I felt like I was running on a treadmill inside a tornado, and no matter how fast I ran, I could not keep up—and all the while, life was spinning faster and faster. Go faster, try harder, look better—all at the same time—is just too much for anyone to accomplish.

Instead of saying to myself, *This is insane, just stop it*, I decided the answer was to call in reinforcements. Get a little outside help to do what I needed to do in order to go faster, try harder, and look better. Enter: cocaine.

So, in essence, this is the story of a girl who tried too hard and used too much to have too much; but, by losing it all, she found herself—and became the woman she was destined to be.

> *Let us not look backward in anger, or forward in fear, but around in awareness.*
>
> **—James Thurber**

I'm Going as Fast as I Can!

Awareness does not happen when you're trapped in an illusion—or when you're living each day at a hundred miles an hour but feeling like you're at a dead stop. You long to scream, "I'm going as fast as I can!" But you don't. You can't scream, and you can't stop, because no one will listen and no one will care.

When life has become a competition, you automatically feel alone—it is you against the world, with no one to cheer for you and no one to care. Only you care, because you want to win. It isn't until you realize that we each are winners—and losers—at one time or another that you can feel okay if you don't "win."

Part of getting to that place means acknowledging that anything that anyone feels at any moment in time has been felt by at least one other person at some point in time. There is nothing new under the sun; yet, simultaneously, life is filled with infinite possibilities and choices. This very dichotomy is exactly what makes life amazing and beautiful and scary and unpredictable. Because of that, it is also what helps us recognize that we are never alone—not really. There is always something—or someone—to reach out to that will let us know we each and all are part of life and the universe.

At the end of the day, all we can do is live—as best we can. Some days will just be better than others, and some days, *we'll* just be better than we are on other days. And some days, putting one foot in front of the other is all we can do. On those days, maybe we do need to say out loud: "I'm going as fast as I can!" It doesn't matter if anyone else hears or cares, but it does matter that we do. If we don't care for ourselves, no matter who else does care for us, it will never be enough.

Contemporary affluent America says that women can do it all and have it all—and it's just that easy. I guarantee I am not alone in feeling that not just "keeping up" but also "maintaining" is extremely hard to do. I know this, because, while attending my groups of wine club, book club, French club, baby French club, and baby gym, I could sense the tension in the air. It wasn't until I joined a new-mommy play-date group that I was offered cocaine for the first time. Yes, you heard me correctly: *I was offered cocaine in a new-mommies group.*

So it was not outrageous that I thought I had found "the answer." Obviously, a lot of other women just like me thought they had found it, too. Until that fateful moment, I had always wondered how these women could keep up their homes, cart kids around to every extracurricular activity you could think of, meet for tennis matches, travel, maintain salon hairdos, look Photoshop perfect—and still find time to deliver fantastic homemade cupcakes to every single elaborate play date.

I would soon come to find out how all this was possible. Translation: *It was achievable because these mommies were high on cocaine.*

But I digress; back to how it actually started for me. One day at my new-mommies group, as I was striking up a conversation about how we all needed more hours in the day, a fellow new mommy took me aside to make an incredible offer. When I say "incredible," I mean it in the truest sense of the word. I literally could not believe what she said to me.

"Brienne, I'm telling you, this is the answer to your prayers. We *all* do it."

I listened in utter shock and disbelief as I watched her take a makeup pouch out of her diaper bag and rummage around until she produced a tiny plastic bag of white powder. I knew instantly what it was. I was speechless, but I kept thinking, So that's *how they all do it—the running around, the perfect homes, the perfect hair, the perfect kids . . . the fantastic cupcakes.*

"Brienne?"

I mumbled something utterly forgettable in response; I can't remember exactly what it was. It might have just been, "Hmmm?"

"Before you decide you don't want to, just try it. You won't believe how fantastic it is! What else do you know of that can take away stress *and* give you energy? It isn't like you're going to become a drug addict, for goodness sake! It just helps . . ."

Her voice trailed off. I can't tell you for sure if she said something else that I just don't remember or if she stopped talking. What I can tell you is that, in my mind, I was hooked on the possibility before I even got hooked on cocaine. What else could offer relief from stress *and* increase energy? Nothing I had ever heard of. *What overscheduled mom wouldn't be interested in the miracle she offered?* I thought. If there were any, I didn't know them—and I wasn't one of them. It sounded fantastic to me as I watched her eyes glitter over the little baggie she proffered. Fantastic. Just like all those cupcakes were. Just like I was going to be.

Okay. I've already admitted to using it and becoming addicted. In case you're wondering, "How did that just happen?" let's just cut right to the chase: I was not exactly what could be called an angel in the illegal-substance department during my college years. I am not making excuses for what I did then or what I did as an overwhelmed new mommy. However, the difference between college and mommies groups is that drinking and drugging between tests and finals is one thing; drinking and drugging between diaper changes is another. Quite another.

Yet, as that baggie filled with powdery snow was offered to me, all that it promised was too hard to resist. This was a very surreal moment as I teetered on the fine line between reality and insanity. The reality was that I needed a boost that would also help me learn to de-stress over time, and this sounded like a harmless little jump-start/soothe combo. The insanity was twofold: first, that handing out cocaine in a new-mommies group had somehow become an acceptable notion and commonplace occurrence; and second, that I was so overwhelmed, I thought it sounded like a good and reasonable idea.

Part of the reason I felt it was reasonable was that I realized I was not alone in feeling overwhelmed by the quest to put on the perfect exterior. We were a group of women who not only put ourselves aside for every call of duty but who had also lost ourselves in the shuffle. If only more of us— maybe even just one of us—had stood up in that group and honestly said, "Is anyone else as exhausted as I am? What are we doing? And why?"

But no one did, including me. It's so much easier to think that something or someone—or anything or anyone—can do it for us. Then we can keep up, look great, impress, and have fun . . . and that is much more appealing than facing our fears, taking care of ourselves, and really and truly growing up. It seems that way at the start, anyway.

Striving for excellence motivates you; striving for perfection is demoralizing.

—Harriet Braiker

Sugar-Coated Goodness

I kept looking at the baggie in her hand. It felt like I had been looking at it for a long time, but I couldn't have been, because she didn't say anything else. She didn't need to. I wouldn't have heard anything she said at that point. I didn't really see her anymore, either. I didn't see anything but that bag. Actually, that's not completely accurate. What I saw was the promise that the bag held. The promise of the endless energy it would deliver. The countless fantastic cupcakes I would create. The promise that it would help me escape to a place where I would have peace.

No human being has or can sustain an endless amount of energy, but we each have the potential for an amazing amount of energy, in spite of our needing rest and nutrition and nurturing to restore ourselves. Beyond that, peace is not found in a place you escape to; peace is found in your heart, and only you can cultivate it there.

But I had to find these things out the hard way.

The white powder looked so pristine and perfect in the baggie, like a first snowfall or confectioner's sugar on delicate pastries. The kind I'd be using soon for my to-die-for cupcakes.

Then, just as the image crystallized in my mind, it evaporated. Every thought and judgment left my mind. All I could think about was how much energy I would have to tackle the myriad activities that I needed to accomplish in the course of my insanely jam-packed day. Fantastic cupcakes were the least of it.

Let me back up again for a minute to explain what it is like to be a first-time mommy with twins. If there is one thing that's true about twins, it's that they have an inordinate amount of energy. Once they reach toddlerhood, that energy transforms itself into one thing: speed. Mathematically, twins might equal two toddlers, but to their mommy, it can feel like taking care of four, or even six, little ones. Inevitably, the moment you catch one and get situated, the other streaks past, and upon capture, you are sure to discover that the first one is now gone, and so on.

Suffice it to say that I always felt like the ringleader of a miniature circus. But, if my energy—and thereby, speed—could match my kids' . . . well, that would be a different story. I would be able to manage the house and all my outside clubs and activities, take care of the twins, prepare fabulous meals—and don't forget the cupcakes!—and look gorgeous, with not so much as a hair out of place, when my husband came home from work.

Hmmm, I thought. *The baggie and its magical promise, or an endless stream of exhausting days, one after the other, with no end in sight. Kind of a no-brainer.* Let me just add that, at the time, my son was enduring an excessive number of appointments in an attempt to get him caught up with other kids in his age group (about 2 years old): occupational therapist, speech therapist, physical therapist, feeding group, and sign-language instructor. Although some people consider premature babies to be cute and tiny, what they fail to comprehend are the repercussions of being born too soon. My twins were born very prematurely and remained in the hospital until each one was stable enough to come home. From the very start of this journey, I had stress up to my eyeballs and felt like I was having an anxiety attack every day. Couple that feeling with an over-the-top lactation nurse—worse than any nun in my Catholic high school—who made me feel like a failure, and I was brewing up a major disaster. Why did she make me feel like a failure? This nurse told me that breastfeeding them at the same time was simple, and she just couldn't understand what my problem was. Well, managing a breastfeeding pose called the "double football hold" with two squirming babies is an urban legend not unlike perfectly folding a fitted sheet. It cannot be done.

Needless to say, all the appointments for my son were worth it, because he is now developmentally caught up with everyone else. As I would discover later, some things that were thought to be wrong with him were actually early signs that he was more on track than I ever could have imagined at the time. It's one of those things I look back on now that make me realize how far I had my head up my rear.

But back to my first sniff. I'm not relating this to make excuses for my choices, just to show all the details of my life, which, when combined on a daily basis, made me feel that I couldn't cope with my life as it was.

It was just too much for me to handle on my own. I needed something to help me get through the day. At the time, I told myself that everybody did—and the prevalence of cocaine at the new-mommies group validated that feeling. I guess we all had our heads pretty far up our rears.

The fact remains that I couldn't see that things would get better; that I'd find my own pace and my own comfort zone as a mom and as a wife—and as a person. All I could see was that I had to keep up with everyone else. And if that were the case, why shouldn't I avail myself of the same thing that helped everyone else maintain that insane pace in the first place? So, of course I jumped at the opportunity to hit the cocaine and wait for a mad rush of energy.

I took the baggie, never realizing that the course of my life would change forever.

With any drug, at first, you experience the honeymoon period, when everything is fantastic and wonderful. In fact, the only question you ask yourself is, *Why are more people not trying this?* There is an adrenaline rush—your energy does increase exponentially in the beginning. And there is also a sense of euphoria that feels like peace. All these positive feelings blend with one another in the beginning, and you just cannot stop marveling at how good you feel—how great life is. If only you'd found out about this magical option sooner!

After my first sniff, I was on my way to getting more accomplished in a day than Martha Stewart in the halcyon days before you-know-what. Just as I had envisioned, fantastic play-date cupcakes could be made in the same day as tackling housework, taking care of the twins, running errands, shopping, cooking dinner, and still looking fabulous when my husband arrived home from work.

Translation: *Yes, cupcakes for me and cupcakes for all! Hallelujah for cupcakes and cocaine!*

Mountains cannot be surmounted except by winding paths.

—Johann Wolfgang von Goethe

Cash, Check, or Charge?

Once an addict is hooked, he or she will go to any lengths to maintain the addiction. It takes over your life, your thoughts, and, eventually, your soul. Some of us are able to find all the pieces, put ourselves back together, and reclaim ourselves and our lives—or make new ones. I was fortunate enough to be able to. Others are not so lucky.

In retrospect, I realize that, at least for me, the ease with which I was able to maintain my addiction was a big part of the reason why I became addicted in the first place. I'm not saying I wouldn't have anyway, but it's being as easy as it was just made it, well, easy. Too easy.

I don't waste time or energy wishing it hadn't been that easy. Wishing away the past, and our actions in it, has no purpose. All that just leads to nonproductive grief and angst and negativity; we have to move forward. Nevertheless, when we're in the thick of it, it doesn't ever hurt to gently remind ourselves that things that seem too good to be true usually are. And cocaine—and the way I obtained mine—certainly falls into that category.

How did she get it, anyway? If that's what you're thinking, you're not alone. Whenever I share information about my addiction, curiosity has always arisen as to where I got my drug supply. I think most people had a notion that I was meeting my connection in dark alleys or under a bridge, or that I was traveling deep into a labyrinth-like urban ghetto. That could not be further from the truth, which is why it made it all too easy to get.

You hear about the type of drug dealer who pulls up in a van on a street corner; or maybe you watch a lot of cop shows on TV. That's not the only way to make a connection. There are dealers a step above those shadier types. My personal dealer, Steve, was very friendly and clean-cut and had the kind of outgoing personality that made you want to be friends with him. Never once did I feel awkward, sleazy, or unsafe when I dropped by his place for a pickup.

Steve was like the Iron Chef of buying and selling cocaine—he accepted personal checks and money orders for his clients' convenience. If he had time to chat, you'd come in and he'd weigh out a bag for you while he checked his Facebook page, or made music CDs, or did whatever else he was doing at the time. It was all pretty casual and matter-of-fact. Over and above that, it wasn't really a place you imagined you'd go to buy drugs; however, he'd cut a few lines while you waited to "make you feel better." If he had lined up several customers in a day at close proximity to one another time-wise, then he would "mat you." That meant he'd leave your order under his doormat; you picked it up, left cash, and then texted him that you had your stuff and had left the money.

I always assumed that he put it under his doormat because he was gone, which baffled me, since it seemed like that cash could be under the mat for a long time. Finally I figured out—quite by accident, I might add—that he was actually home and doing multiple sales. Steve was quite a business-minded kind of guy.

I happened to arrive earlier than my specified time, only to find a pile of cash and no cocaine under his mat. I was very surprised, because that meant that someone was just ahead of me, still picking up their order. Even when customers were scheduled back-to-back, necessitating that Steve "mat me," I had never actually arrived when someone else was still there completing a transaction.

I called him from my cell. "Hey, Steve. I'm a little early, but there's only cash under the mat."

"Hey, Brienne," he said. "Just hang tight in your car for a bit. My 'real seven o'clock' is here."

"'kay," I said and flipped my phone shut. While I waited out back, I happened to notice that his "real" appointment looked just like a local TV personality. He strode out of Steve's place, hopped into a hot little sports car, and drove off. I desperately wanted to ask Steve if that was, indeed, who I thought it was. I resisted the urge, though, because I knew that Steve was excellent about privacy and keeping things under wraps.

However, by my calculations, during a span of about forty-five minutes while I was "hanging tight" in my car, Steve had made somewhere around a thousand dollars. It could have been more, but I based my calculations on my purchase, what I saw under the mat, and how much Mr. TV might have purchased.

Steve's earning capacity certainly correlated to his customers' addictions—mine and others'; it was financially worth his while to keep us hooked. That's true for every drug dealer. It doesn't have anything to do with my recovery. I don't blame Steve or hold him responsible in any way. I made the choice, and I continued to make it every time I called him to score. He didn't do me any favors by making it easy and convenient, but it didn't seem that way at the time. It doesn't really matter. We shouldn't make significant choices because they seem easy, or avoid them because they seem hard. We should make the right choices the right way, especially when they're significant ones—and, more often than not, the right way is not the easy way. That's just how life is.

But remember that the toughest lessons, and the hardest-won wisdom, are the things that stay with us.

Whenever you fall, pick up something.
—**Oswald Theodore Avery**

All Honeymoons Must End

I have to be honest: There was a step between smoking weed in college and sniffing cocaine at the new-mommies group. A step on the path to addiction, I mean. It was painkillers. Muscle relaxants. All things that were prescribed or recommended by my doctor. But when you have a predisposition for addiction, there is only a fine line between a reasonable need for enough help to get through something difficult and the all-consuming obsession of never having enough. Addicts don't teeter on that line—they don't even just cross it—they pole-vault over it. Addicts plunge into waters where nonaddicts would never dare to even dip a toe.

It began ordinarily enough. Lots of women endure severe physical pain and discomfort during pregnancy, childbirth, and afterward. I was no exception. As a result of pregnancy and the birth of premature twins, needless to say, my body had endured many physical challenges. While I was pregnant, my back often just "went out" because of postural changes and weight shifts—all the result of carrying twins. After the twins were born, I constantly had two squirming little ones who needed to be carried and cared for. Don't get me wrong—I loved caring for them; it's just that I was suddenly required to lift and bend in ways I hadn't known were possible. And my body certainly hadn't known it! Needless to say, back pain, as well as migraine pain resulting from pinched nerves, began to take a toll.

To make a long story short, what started out as a few muscle relaxants and painkillers quickly became an addiction to medication, "quickly" being the operative word. I am not exaggerating when I say it happened so fast that I didn't even realize it. I didn't feel myself becoming addicted. One minute, I was taking the meds because I needed to dull the pain; the next, I was taking them because it was the only way I could get through the day. This is just the way addiction happens.

To describe it in a more clinical/scientific way, tolerance is usually built up with the use of any type of drug. When I began using prescription painkillers for back pain and headaches, one here and there would do the trick. As the back and headache pain continued, so did the pill usage; I soon needed two or three in order to feel any relief. To pick up on what I said earlier, before you can say, "mail-order prescription drugs from Canada," you're knee-deep in it with a very high tolerance. I hadn't realized that the pain pills, because I was taking them so often, were causing more of a problem than they were solving; simply put, it became a vicious cycle that became increasingly difficult to stop. It wasn't until I entered rehab that I was able to totally detoxify my body from being dependent on the pills *and* on cocaine.

I had previously tried to quit on my own, but I always gave up as soon as I felt too miserable to make it through a day without them. That, by the way, is the classic, telltale sign of addiction: You cannot get through even a day without the substance (or behavior) that you are addicted to. In my case, having small twins and a hectic schedule left me no time to quit by myself. Again, no excuses—that is just the way it was, or, at least, the way I felt about it. When you believe that other things—whatever they might be—are more important than taking care of yourself, it's a whole lot easier to just have another drink, pop another pill, snort another line, than it is to do what you need to do to take care of yourself. It's easier to keep doing what you've been doing—which, let's face it, is "working" for you—than it is to stop. (Once in rehab, I could rest after feeling nauseated, and I could sleep when feeling weak and exhausted. But I'm getting ahead of my own story. More on rehab later.)

But how did she get to that to point? How did she get addicted? Depending upon why you're reading this book, you might be wondering how I got to that point, or about how you got there yourself, or about how someone you care about who's in the midst of the same kind of struggle I went through got there; regardless, the answer is pretty much the same. I didn't just "get" to that point. No one does. The same way that no one ever just "dabbles" in mind-altering substances. Addiction is the result of abuse, and abuse is not "dabbling." Abuse is the misuse of something, usually something that is not good for you in the first place. I mean, no one abuses broccoli or mineral water.

But saying that I didn't just "get" to that point is only part of the answer. When I began "dabbling" (that's how I thought of it at the time, "dabbling" to take the edge off the pain so I could get through the day and take care of my house and my kids) with prescription drugs and cocaine, I was living the life of champagne wishes and cocaine dreams. I was doing what I needed to do to rise above the pain and carry on with my life. (Even though I was being selfish while using drugs, I never exposed my kids to it. They never saw me use and because I was not able to breastfeed for longer than their first four days of life, I did spare them in several ways.) For everyone else, I was being superwoman and supermom. Family members were patting me on the back because I was tearing through my days like lightning, with tons of energy and a bright smile at day's end.

That was only on the outside. On the inside, which they couldn't see, I was falling apart faster than I could handle—faster than I ever could have imagined would be possible before I entered the parallel universe of drug abuse. Drug abuse first engendered, and then magnified, my feelings of self-hate, low confidence, and failure. It magnified them by the minute. I was so ashamed of what I was doing behind closed doors that I never would have been able to muster the courage to ask for help. I was deeply ashamed of the person I had allowed myself to become, and I felt I couldn't own up to the responsibility of telling the truth. Nevertheless, throughout that whole time, I was secretly pleading for help and support, even as I fought as hard as I could to not let my façade crack.

Throughout the duration of my drug abuse, it never once occurred to me that I was plunging myself deeper and deeper into the hard-core realm of drugs. It has been said that cocaine use died out with the eighties, but I have to disagree. Cocaine starts as a social thing, kind of like how smoking weed was in college. You invited people over to smoke a bowl with you, shared joints, and bonded over your mutual drug use. Cocaine seemed to be the mature, expensive version of weed. We shared cocaine at nightclubs and parties; we invited people into public bathroom stalls to join in; always, we bonded over our mutual drug use. You would be shocked at the number of invites to join in—and even more so by the number that accepted.

Once, in a bathroom stall, I was introduced to a woman who, coincidentally, was married to a childhood friend of mine. Unfortunately, I know that my friend had no clue that his wife was a closet coke user. The sad fact was that she and I were blindly introduced—if you can call cramming into a public restroom stall an introduction—and, again, by sheer coincidence, I figured out who she was. *Don't worry, Jane; your secret is safe with me*, I thought. Unfortunately, cocaine did not go out with the eighties. My story and countless others prove that it is alive and thriving.

Crashing through and banging around life with drug addiction on your back feels like you are trying to perform a graceful ballet while wearing chains with cement blocks hanging from them. At the beginning, it seemed like a graceful ballet, and it was beautiful. But then, as the beauty and grace became weighted down by the addiction, it degenerated, all too soon. It became painful, glaring, and loud. And then, just as quickly, it fell silent. Frighteningly so.

I would be the first one to admit that, as the addiction and abuse took control during those drug- and alcohol-laden months, life was not very pretty. And neither was I. I am not talking about outward appearances. Being the closet drug addict that I was, I never let the people I loved, or anyone around me, know what was going on. As I've said, outwardly, I kept it pretty together. My husband and family had no clue, and I never let my kids see anything.

Still, like attracts like; at that time, I was attracting people who were just as lost and messed up as I was. Even then, I was certainly not proud of the things I did, the people I hung out with, or how I treated my family—unbeknownst to any of them. I don't blame my ex-husband for divorcing and hating me. At that time, I deeply hated myself, too. But I have to be honest: I was not the one who decided to put an end to my drug abuse. Even with all the pain and self-loathing that come with the territory, addicts stay hooked. It takes guts and strength to get unstuck. But it can be done. You can do it. "Where there's a will, there's a way," might sound corny, but it's true. Stand tall. Be strong. Make it happen.

Life is what we make it. Always has been; always will be.
—Grandma Moses

All Aboard, Captain

The moment of truth always comes. The longer we put it off, the harder it is to face. The more we avoid facing it, the harder it is to deal with when we have to.

Life is filled with choices. We make them—small and large—every day. Choosing to not make a choice is also a choice. And every choice we make has a consequence. Sometimes we can anticipate the consequences, and the choices we make are simply our way of avoiding consequences we'd rather not deal with. Other times we can't foresee the consequences. But they are there. And they find us.

As a rule, the consequences of the choices we should not have made in the first place are the worst ones we ever have to deal with.

I would be the first person to tell you that cocaine falls into that category. And the honeymoon choice was not worth the hell of consequences that came after.

Every morning when I woke up, I tried to bury the immediate waves of fear, anxiety, exhaustion, stress, denial, and depression. I tried, but I always failed. So then I would start to bargain with myself about my cocaine use. This bargaining practice was so regular that I felt like I could get a job as an auctioneer. The "dialogue" between my "inner auctioneer" and me went something like this:

Do I hear a, "Throw the cocaine away and own up to the truth?"

I have a, "No, I need one more line to get through today, and then I'll stop."

Over in the corner, I hear, "You need more cocaine (than one line) today so you don't feel like crap."

"Aha! Going once. Going twice. Sold! Final bid goes to the painfully oblivious mother in need of help."

I really did fight a mental battle every moment of the day, trying to accept the terrible hand of cards I had dealt myself. I wanted so desperately to tell someone or ask for help, but, as I've described, I just could not get past the fear of failure. I had convinced myself that, if I admitted my problems, I would disappoint everyone in my life and let them all down. After all, everyone assumed I was organized, content, satisfied, and complete—so much so that I sort of became a caricature of myself. I played the role of who I was supposed to be every day. It became so automatic that, at the time, I didn't realize that I had turned myself into this character; but it wasn't me—it was others' projections of me. Deep down, I never wanted anything more than to not be a failure and to make others happy.

The worst of it was that I felt I was failing myself. Even the cocaine abuse couldn't mask the truth of that. I needed superhuman energy because I couldn't stand going through the motions of existing as me anymore. There was no me anymore—not the me I had always been and known, anyway.

Sure, I had once been happy with my husband, children, and lifestyle. My general outlook was one of optimism. But, all too quickly, I became extremely *un*happy, even though I denied that fact to myself. What made me unhappy were the self-induced pressures I visited upon myself in my struggle to "keep up" and appear "fabulous" all the time. This perpetuated an endless cycle of anxiety, stress, inadequacy—and, most of all, loneliness. It's pretty hard *not* to feel unhappy with all of that going on nonstop in your head, no matter how much "junk" you take in to numb out.

Cocaine abuse made it all worse. That's the ultimate irony: What I used to make it all bearable only made it all worse. Much worse. The deeper I dove into my addiction, the more I distanced myself from everyone in my life—including myself. In retrospect, I think I pushed myself farther away than I pushed anyone else.

Marianne Williamson's *A Woman's Worth* sums it up well, I think:

More women cry, loudly or silently, every fraction of every moment, in every town of every country, than anyone—man or woman—realizes. We cry for our children, our lovers, our parents, and ourselves. We cry in shame because we feel no right to cry, and we cry in peace because we feel it's time we did cry. We cry in moans and we cry in great yelps. We cry for the world. Yet we think we cry alone. We feel that no one hears.

As alone as I felt, other women were feeling overwhelmed by the same pressures that overwhelmed me. I recognized that, considering the fact that I was first offered cocaine at a new-mommies group. *Hello-o-o.* What I didn't see was that all of us in that group could have, and should have, reached out to one another instead of reaching for cocaine.

But when we disconnect from ourselves, we feel alone, regardless of where we are and who we are with. We feel alone because we can't find ourselves—we've lost touch with the core of what makes us, *us.* We feel alone, but we are not alone. We weren't alone at all, those women in my new-mommies group and me; we were unconsciously bonded to one another by a sense of familiarity, even though our camaraderie was filled with confusion and uncertainty. Without even knowing it, we were all on board together. We should have tried to reach out to one another, to share our pain and fears, instead of trying to mask and hide them.

We were like people adrift on a sinking ship, with a lifeboat just within reach—except that our lifeboat was ourselves and one another, and we just couldn't see it. I could have jumped into the lifeboat, but I was afraid it would sink. Instead, I clung harder to the sinking ship. Finally, someone sank my sinking ship, and I thank God for that. I hate to imagine where I'd be if that sinking ship hadn't been sunk for good. There was no way I was jumping into that lifeboat.

No matter how far you have gone on a wrong road, turn back.
—Turkish Proverb

2

The Big Bang Theory

Look and Learn—Bang!

Self-reflection. Hmmm. What does it really mean? It means more than just looking in the mirror, regardless of how we feel about what we see. It's a big concept—a huge concept; we all know that. But, again, what does it *really* mean? Can any of us look at ourselves and really see who we are? Do we see a kind of version of what others see, or do we see a deeper part of ourselves that no one else sees, because no one else can ever see our true selves?

I don't think there is one right or simple answer to any of these questions. But, in some extraordinary moments, we do get a glimpse of who we really are—and then it is up to each of us whether we accept and make peace with that, or reject and struggle against it. Regardless of what we do as a result of these extraordinary moments and glimpses, sooner or later, we have to make a choice about self-reflection. Make no mistake: Never self-reflecting is also a choice.

Don't laugh, but I first saw my true self because of a pair of white sandals. To be honest, at the time I didn't know what I was seeing—or that I was seeing anything, for that matter. I only knew I hurt like hell. It seemed as if the heat of my own anger would burn me up in that moment. Part of me almost welcomed that, because then I would disappear; if I disappeared, I wouldn't have to face the pain—or do the work. But now, when I think back on that moment, I realize I was seeing my true self, not *in* the sandals, but *through* them, because of what they represented and showed me about myself.

Seeing ourselves as we are, and accepting ourselves as we are, takes time and courage. The first step is realizing that we *need* to see and accept ourselves as we are. That did not happen easily for me; I guess it doesn't for anyone, but I can speak only for myself. It came to me with a jolt; or, more precisely, a bang. A big bang. But first, back to the shoes—the white sandals.

My first reaction when I saw those white sandals was, *How tacky! It's after Labor Day, you twit.* I was enraged that "she"—the still-nameless "she"—was staying over often enough to leave her shoes at my ex-husband's house. I was on fire knowing that my beautiful twins were caught in the middle of two adults who were falling apart before their innocent, young eyes. Worse yet, those two adults were their parents: my ex and me. But even more than that, the hard truth of it was this: I was angry that he had found someone to step into my place so quickly. Although it had been months and the kids were now age 3, it seemed as if only hours had passed since we had fallen apart.

You know what? Screw you, White Shoes. You can have him, and you can keep him; I don't care. I hope you live it up, baby. You know what's going to happen in the end? You're going to get absolutely nothing. That's right, nothing—the same thing I got. Congratulations! Cheers! Good luck to you! I'm better off without him. Much better.

Those were my thoughts the day I went to pick up my kids at my ex-husband's house. I didn't encounter "her" at that point. Nothing had actually happened. My young son had merely brought me her white sandals to try on, the innocent action of a child. Of course, it wasn't about the shoes, white or otherwise. It was simply that it had never occurred to me that my ex would have a girlfriend so fast, let alone one who left her shoes at his house—because a woman would do that only if she came over frequently enough not to miss her shoes at her own house. And let me clarify that this was not just my ex's house. This was *our* house—our home, his and mine. Or, at least, it had been. This was the home that he and I built together, the place where we started our family—the place where we fell apart. But even so, it was still ours. To me, anyway.

Anger is a galvanizer for most people, and it galvanized me. Seeing those white sandals brought me up short, but my rage in the wake of it clarified certain things. For starters, I realized that what I was feeling, including the present anger, was something I had asked for—practically begged for, to be honest. I deserved every hurtful and disastrous thing coming to me. After all, I was the one who cheated. I was the one who embraced another and let that other come between my husband and me. In other words, I was the one who emotionally, physically, and spiritually checked out. I was the one who selfishly hurt and destroyed innocent bystanders, including my children. I was the one who hurt and destroyed the witnesses to my destruction, who included me. I was pretty much my only witness, because I had hidden what I was doing from everyone but myself. Karma was a real bitch.

In retrospect, I now know exactly what happened. At that very moment, standing in the house and staring at her fashion-backward white sandals, I felt and experienced exactly what my ex had felt when he discovered me with another. I felt what he had felt: anger, resentment, disbelief, disgust, sadness, and more hot, intense anger. What I was witnessing was a blatant display of not accepting any responsibility for my actions. I had focused all the blame on him, while remaining blind to how I had been the one—the only one—who made all this happen. In my mind I was saying to this woman, *Good. You can have him, and you can keep him. Just wait and see how he's going to treat you. Just wait and see how he's going to make you feel. Just wait.*

Bang! For the first time, I could look at how I had treated him—and really see it. When we cheat on someone we promised to love and cherish through thick and thin, we also cheat on ourselves. I am not proud of my affair or my drug abuse, but I accept responsibility for both—and I recognize that both reflected my inability to accept and love myself. That is not an excuse or a justification; it is the honest truth, and revealing it is not easy. Prior to witnessing the repercussions of the pain I had inflicted on my ex, I could not fully understand the pain I had inflicted inwardly—how much I had damaged myself by not cherishing my own integrity, and instead, convincing myself that quick fixes would get me through the life I had created but could no longer manage.

At this point, I was not as aware as I am now, and much of what I just described I would not fully understand for a while. In the instant that I saw the shoes, though, I felt the pain—and it forced me to examine my actions and their far-reaching effects on me and on others. I had yet to understand how important our individual roles are within the universe. In short, this was to be but one of many painful lessons on how things in life really work.

My ex instinctively had created an exact mirror image for me. Not only did I hate that I saw myself, but I also refused to acknowledge it. I loathed and was disgusted by what I saw. Whether in spite of or because of that, I sank deep into it.

Carrying around those feelings for weeks was beginning to take a major toll on me. It wasn't until I went to visit my therapist, Dr. Dani, that I began to understand what was happening. Dr. Dani explained something very profound. She said, "It's not until it happens to you that you truly understand it." Big bang!

It was, indeed, happening to me, and I was finally able to understand and acknowledge the part of myself I still continued to hate and ignore.

The moment I accepted that I had created everything that had happened to me—yes, everything—my healing process began. And, yes, I did accept it in a single moment of pure clarity. Unintentionally, my ex's actions allowed me to see myself and how I had affected my family, friends, and relationships—but, even more important, how I had compromised my own integrity, as I described above.

I finally discovered and acknowledged that, yes, I was at the bottom—and I was the only one who had gotten me there. Very big bang!

The universe is full of magical things patiently waiting for our wits to grow sharper.

—Eden Phillpotts

When Enough Is Really Enough

We have already established that self-reflection is about more than just looking in the mirror. Okay, a lot more. More than almost anything else, self-reflection requires honesty—no, it actually demands it. Without honesty, self-reflection is pointless. And part of honest self-reflection is knowing when enough is enough. For anyone with addiction challenges, this is a huge concept. It takes tremendous effort for an addict to reconcile this within himself or herself, and even more effort to master it and put it into practice every day.

Simply put, addicts are missing the "enough switch" that nonaddicts take for granted. Part of recovery must involve finding, and using, that switch. Easier said than done.

Most addicts need to hit rock bottom before they are truly and honestly ready to recover and heal. This is because addicts lack the enough switch—each individual addict may have additional reasons, but these are layered on top of this lack. People who have the enough switch have little, if any, chance of becoming addicts. Addiction is an all-or-nothing mind-set:

The motivating need to escape reality and the need to crash back to earth in order to clean up one's act and "get it" are opposite sides of the same coin.

Only after addicts hit rock bottom can they find and effectively use the enough switch. Here is the story of how I found and learned to use mine.

Before rehab, when I heard people say that a person wouldn't get it until he or she hit rock bottom, I always assumed that meant the person would have to be living in his or her car, with nothing at all. I assumed rock bottom meant losing everything, including your teeth.

In a sense, I did lose everything, even though I still had all my teeth—I even had a retainer. I lost trust, love, and safety; I lost my family; most of all, I lost my self-respect. The material things disappeared, as well, including the house, the retirement fund, the eight-hundred-thread-count sheets, and one incredible vacuum cleaner.

Oddly enough, it was this vacuum cleaner that taught me how to find and use my enough switch. (In case you're wondering, there was nothing wrong with the switch on the vacuum!)

My ex had bought me a very expensive Dyson vacuum that I dearly loved. (I really do enjoy vacuuming.) When he packed up my things and moved me out of the house, he certainly did not give me the Dyson. Because I was trying to save money, I did not purchase a new vacuum right away; instead, I used a sticky-tape lint roller. (Okay, this time I know you're laughing. You can stop. The tape actually picks up more than you might think.)

The point is, it didn't matter how low I sank; I insisted on having a clean environment. I guess it's kind of a variation on making lemonade out of lemons, except that my version was, "If life gives you lemons, make a lemon-drop martini, and then conjure up a vacuum cleaner out of a lint roller." I admit that the first part stemmed from my not yet being completely sober; the last part was the result of watching a lot of *MacGyver* episodes. The important part of that realization was that I finally got it—it was time for me to climb up from the bottom. Time to reclaim my life. No one could do it for me; I had to do it myself.

I never had the feeling of, *Okay, I've had enough, and I'm moving on.* Remember, I don't have an enough switch, so I had to hit bottom to get the "that's enough" message that nonaddicts receive and understand without giving it a second thought. For me, the message that resulted from hitting bottom was more a crystal-clear feeling of, *Okay, I see the lesson I must learn, and I will accept a new learning process.*

As soon as I saw and accepted that, I realized I was on the right path. Plus, what I really needed was to accept my fears and learn to adapt. It felt like I was diving into uncharted territory of experiences, emotions, and outcomes. It seemed that way to me at the time because I didn't have a framework for what was happening to me. I didn't realize, and couldn't possibly have known, that I felt fearful, shaky, and vulnerable *because* I was on the right track—as difficult as that might be to believe. And when I felt it, I wouldn't have believed it, either. Fortunately, I didn't overthink it; I just trusted my gut. The more I contemplated what was ahead, the more I trusted my instincts; I intuitively sensed that I was being guided down the right path. There is no other way to explain how I felt or how things turned out. Sometimes I wished the angels would have just taken out an ad in the paper or bought a billboard to get the point across. My apologies to my guardian angel, who probably never thought to ask for overtime or vacation days, but surely earned them looking out for me. I guess not asking for things like that is part of how a guardian angel is picked in the first place, but I am grateful.

> Great trouble comes from not knowing enough. Great conflict arises from wanting too much. When we know when enough is enough, there will always be enough.
> —*Tao Te Ching*

Clark Kent and Superman

Only after honest self-reflection can we start to change in a positive way. This is true for everyone. And it's hard for everyone. But, for former addicts, it's almost impossible. For former addicts, it is superhuman. I am not exaggerating.

Unfortunately, unlike superheroes, we don't have superhuman powers and/or props to help us manage these superhuman feats. Think about it: Clark Kent had that phone booth. Could he have pulled off turning into the Man of Steel without it? We don't have old-fashioned phone booths we can jump into in order to effect a flawless switcheroo—one that changes not only our outfits but our very selves, eliminating our fears, doubts, and limitations in the same magical instant that it changes a business suit into a superhero costume.

We don't have that, but we do have something else Clark Kent had: courage. That's right, courage. A superhero has to have courage, and so does his or her alter ego. Clark Kent—and even Superman—did have to deal with a piece of kryptonite or two. That took courage. Knowing that no matter how strong we become, we still have to show up and live every day takes courage, too. The only way we can do it is to learn that we have to find a way to accept our shortcomings so we can live with them. And, if we are honest with ourselves, we can recognize that only by accepting and living with our shortcomings can we become stronger and wiser. That's the real secret to being a superhero, anyway—the costumes are cool, sure, but the ability to perform superhuman feats comes from within.

Change isn't easy for anyone, including Clark Kent. Think of the phone-booth switcheroo described above: Clark Kent only made it look easy to go from uptight and nervous to superhuman. Seeming to just skip past mere human confidence—hard-won by life experience and learning from the mistakes we all make and grow stronger and wiser as a result of having made—good old Clark Kent just ran into a phone booth and ripped off his clothes. He made it seem easy, but it isn't easy for anyone—maybe it wasn't easy for him, either. Maybe he felt uncomfortable—he was in public, after all—but he knew he had to do what he had to do. We all know that. Would any of us run into the phone booth if we could? I'm not so sure. Can you imagine what would happen if I, or anyone else, did that? First of all, good luck finding a phone booth today. Second of all, anyone who didn't get arrested as a result of tearing off all his or her clothes in public would at least feel embarrassed or self-conscious. In any event, I can tell you for certain that I wouldn't have come out of that phone booth exuding self-confidence, human or superhuman.

Up until this point in my life, I had been a God-fearing Catholic who knew only how to grieve for my sins, praying that one day I would make it through the pearly gates to enter heaven. I never thought twice when the Church decided to add or delete ideas. It was never clear what happened to the concept of purgatory. Catholics were always taught that purgatory was similar to a giant waiting room, where souls had to hang out until their sins were forgiven in order to enter heaven. Then, one day, I found out that the Church had "done away with" purgatory. Hmmm. How could the Church just "do away with" a major concept like that? And how come all Catholics didn't get the memo? I mean, if the church could "do away with" purgatory, believe me, I have a whole boatload of things I'd like to "do away with," too. But this is not an anti-Catholic rant. This is about my spiritual journey; there is no right or wrong way to reach God. By God, I mean the higher power of the universe. What matters is that we each realize that God is love, and God loves us—no matter how much we might hate ourselves, and no matter what expression that self-hatred takes. God wants us only to return to love.

When I first began to hear, see, and manifest things on my new spiritual journey, I became more than confused. Confused because I had just done a hell of a lot of sinning, and now an angel was coming to me—did I deserve an angel? Until then, my motto had been something like, *I'm going to hell, anyway; what's one more bag of cocaine?* It's like the old Catholic joke that it would probably be more fun in hell than heaven, because you'd know more people in hell.

My ex always made jokes about the religious restrictions of the Catholic faith, because he didn't practice any religion. He thought the whole thing was hilarious. "Sure," he would say. "You sin your entire life, and then just a quick plea for forgiveness at the end guarantees you a ticket to heaven. Yeah, right." During our marriage, I would defend the Catholic creed when he said that. But, after rehab, I had to agree that I could see where he was coming from.

What's up with all that? I think to myself now. It still blows my mind that I continued to carry shame, guilt, and fear for as long as I did. That is, until I completely and wholly (not holy!) awakened to what was really occurring in the universe. God wants us only to return to love.

> *As soon as you trust yourself, you will know how to live.*
> **—Johann Wolfgang von Goethe**

Dropping the F-Bomb

Self-reflection and change. Change and self-reflection. It's an ongoing cycle. There is a saying that the more things change, the more they stay the same. That doesn't apply to human beings. However, the more we change, the more we grow; the more we grow, the closer we come to connecting with our higher selves—what our souls came into this lifetime to be.

I know that change is constant, and I also know that change is freakin' scary. Who wants to jump into the unknown and wait to be judged or ridiculed? Who wants to patiently twiddle his or her thumbs while waiting to find out what the right thing to do even is? The truth is, no one wants to change because of the *real* four-letter f-word—fear.

Catholics are supposed to live an entire earthbound life avoiding temptation, sin, and all things fun. Again, I'm not Catholic-bashing, but with no religion—or at least without the Catholic religion—a person could live it up his or her entire time on earth and then get a once-over with the magic wand to be ushered right in. That was how it seemed to me, growing up Catholic.

I am a full-blooded Italian American. Imagine the intense fire, fight, and passion for all things in this world—especially pasta. Being born Italian means being born Catholic. Period. That's how it is as far as I know, anyway. Catholic babies come out of the womb automatically bearing faith, belief, guilt, fear, and a few dollar bills for the church basket. I grew up attending a Catholic grade school, and later a hard-core Catholic high school, knowing only devotion, fear of questioning, and itchy wool uniforms.

Asking me to let go of fear was like asking me to pull off a triple-pike, double-loop twisting axel the first time I put on ice skates. You could ask, and I might be willing to try, but I guarantee you it would be ridiculously hard—and the likelihood that I would fall on my face would be pretty good. At least in the beginning.

The point of all this is that, during the process of my spiritual awakening, I was introduced to the philosophical teachings of a man named Osho, who preached modern versions of faith, ideas, and attitudes. When speaking of fear, he said

> . . . peace is to be found only in the midst of pain, and never struggling against or running away from what is considered to be the negative or painful. Yes, cowardice gives you pain, fear gives you pain, anger gives you pain . . . peace can be attained only by accepting the painful, not rejecting it.

What I began to understand was that I had to drop the fear—and also drop who I thought I was—in order to find out who I could become.

> *And the day came when the risk to stay tight in a bud was more painful than the risk it took to blossom.*
>
> **—Anaïs Nin**

3

One Giant Enchilada, Please

Aha Moments

What does it mean to be aware? I mean, really aware—not just of ourselves and those closest to us, or even of the world, but of the whole universe . . . and of being the tiny specks that we are within its vastness? Like all deep questions, this one does not have a real answer, per se.

Life is a journey, but it is also a quest. A quest to discover who we are, what matters most to us, and why we are here. Some people are truly enlightened beings. In a single sacred moment, something deep inside them sings out: *Aha!* That *is why*. And they are aware of their own microscopic status in the vast universe.

This may be the way it happens for the truly enlightened beings who walk among us "regular" people; but I am not sure how many such enlightened ones actually exist. All I can say for sure is that it certainly did not happen that way for me. But what I can also say for sure is that, once you are aware, everything in your life changes—especially you. Quite simply, you are never the same.

We each find our path in our way and in our own time and for our own reasons; the path is different for each of us. What is the same for each of us is that awareness is the first step. If you want to become all you are meant to be, you have to be aware. And, before you can be aware, you have to be awake.

I can tell you the exact moment, day, date, and time when I first awakened to—and then became aware of—the power of the universe. It was when I checked into an in-patient rehab center for drug addiction. Some people say that addicts, alcoholics, and whatever-elses can experience an "aha moment" during rehab. As they describe it, this is supposedly the moment when a light bulb is turned on and the rehab resident gets it—that is, that snorting coke at three in the morning is probably not a good idea, or that drinking to the point of heaving over the porcelain throne is probably not a good idea, either. I'm sure you see where I'm going with this.

I applaud the people who come to that conclusion in a singular moment during their path of cleaning up, whether in rehab or otherwise. However, we don't all see that proverbial light bulb; we don't all get flashes of insight that we can't ignore—that motivate us to change immediately because they are urgent in a unique and undeniable way.

Take me, for instance. I did have an aha moment in rehab, but it was quite different from those light bulbs. It was more of a teeny, tiny voice that said softly, *Hello-o-o-o-o . . . anybody home? You're making the first step of your journey. NOW, like, RIGHT NOW. You . . . yes, you, with the pudding . . . can you hear me?*

I heard the voice, and the best way I can describe it is that it was my own voice, and yet not my own. It was like I knew it was my voice because I recognized it, but I hadn't heard it in so long that I had almost forgotten it existed. It was calling me home—back to myself—despite all odds that I might not listen . . . might not even hear. But I did hear. That's the key: If we hear, we can listen. If we are awake, we can become aware. At some level I intuitively knew this, even though I didn't know that I knew—or know *what* I knew. I just held onto the feeling. I let my intuition direct me to where I needed to go.

I am not looking to romanticize the process in any way. Let me put it this way: My first few days in rehab were hell. Not in the sense of the physical hell of withdrawals, shakes, and vomiting, but more in the sense of the attitudinal hell of the communal bathrooms, sheets, and blankets that creeped me out—coupled with the fact that I was locked up with some real weirdos. I am talking about certifiable crazies. A swanky, posh Promises Center or Clean Valley Rehab this joint was not. No country club *sans* martinis, as I had expected. I was in lockdown with some heavy-hitting heroin junkies, tweakers, and alcoholics. This was the real deal, nothing but the whole enchilada. I was now living with a group of people I would never in my life have associated with on the outside.

At the beginning, I made horrible judgments about the other addicts, the counselors, the nurses, and even the cooks. That's what I meant about the "attitudinal hell" of the communal-living factor. This little country-club girl had ridden in on a white horse, wearing her fantastic shoes (of course—you know by now how much I love my shoes!), and was not about to get down and dirty. Which, given how judgmental I was at the time, meant that I was not about to be "contaminated" by "these addicts."

Part of the lesson I still had to learn was that we were all in the same boat. I might have slept on perfectly laundered eight-hundred-thread-count sheets, while they slept on the street in the middle of who-only-knows what (that I still don't really want to think about), but the fact remained that whatever I once had, and whatever they once had, still left all of us with empty spaces inside that we just couldn't fill. In other words, what we had might be different, but what we were missing was the same, resulting in the emptiness inside and our inability to fill it. That's why we became addicts in the first place. As a consequence, like it or not, I had to share their sheets and bathrooms now—because we were the same. I guess you could say that the beginning of the journey took me from "huh?" to "ewww" to "aha!"

> One's destination is never a place, but rather, a new way of looking at things.
>
> **—Henry Miller**

These Are My Guardian Angels?

Guardian angels do not have halos or wings. (At least they don't when they're earthbound. I guess we'll all have to wait to see what happens when we leave this earth.) No, guardian angels are ordinary people just like you and me. They *look* just like us, anyway. But they are special. Not because they do things that are inordinately heroic or grand or noteworthy, but because they choose to turn their own pain and endured hardships into kindness and help. Instead of becoming bitter as a result of circumstances for which bitterness would be completely understandable, they become kinder and gentler. They reach out to help those in trouble or in pain or afraid, so that such as these do not have to walk alone the way they themselves did.

I was blessed to have not just one but many such guardian angels. And, if I hadn't let go of my own judgments, I might have missed out on all of them. So, keep your eyes, ears, and heart open; remember that such special beings find us when we most need them.

If it hadn't been for my roommate, Tina, I would have bolted out the front door of the rehab facility the morning after I checked in. You had the option to check yourself out, but then, if you ever wanted to come back, it would be next to impossible. Not only would you have bailed on the program, you also would have bailed on the idea of healing yourself.

Tina, a super-cute, well-put-together woman in her mid-fifties, was able to relate well with me. She brought me yogurt when I couldn't eat anything more substantial; she introduced me to people and showed me the ropes; she beat the guys off when they tried to hit on me. In a nutshell, she watched over me, nurturing me and holding my hand the entire time.

One particular event that stands out in my mind was when she straightened out "Gossip Girl"—yeah, there's one wherever you go, even rehab!—who immediately started to dis me to the others before I'd said so much as ten words to any of the other residents but Tina.

"Nobody who's been living on the streets likes a cute nice little girl, Brienne," Tina said softly after Gossip Girl had sniped a remark about how much she could score, drug-wise, off a pair of my shoes.

"But she doesn't even know me!" I protested.

"Of course she doesn't, honey. As far as she's concerned, she doesn't have to. She thinks that if she had all the things she sees that you have, she never would have started using. She doesn't get that we each start using because of an empty place inside that nothing else can fill. It isn't about where you come from or what you have; it's about having lost yourself."

"So, I should give her a pair of my shoes, Tina?" I asked tartly, because I didn't know how to handle the wisdom she'd just shared, not because I was upset with her. What she'd said struck a chord deep inside me, but I wasn't sure quite what to do with it.

"No, smartie. You should just know where she's coming from; acknowledge it, and then let it go. Don't let it get to you. It's easier to hate other people than it is to hate what we wish was different about ourselves."

I nodded. *Wow!* Still struggling to fully embrace and find a way to use her wisdom, I also wondered about something else where Tina was concerned: I couldn't reconcile how she could recognize all that she was sharing with me, yet still need rehab herself.

She gave me a kind of Mona Lisa smile. "I feel the empty place; I just never found anything else to fill it. I know I will, though—I keep trying. If you lose hope, you might as well die. Hope is everything. If you really appreciate what I'm telling you, just don't give up. Don't ever give up." Her voice took on a fierce edge with the last part.

Double wow! I held back tears the same way I knew she did. All I said was, "'kay, Tina."

Tina was, in a word, amazing. To me, the most amazing thing about Tina was that she never once passed judgment on me or anyone else (including Gossip Girl). I think that was why everyone loved Tina—even if they might not have been able to put it into so many words. She was so loving and so open; she was always there for each and every one of us, and she never asked for anything in return.

The best way I can describe it is to say that I loved Tina for the way she treated me, but I respected her for the way she treated everyone. Beyond that, although I wasn't aware of it at the time, Tina was one of my first guiding lights. In hindsight, I realize she was my first guardian angel. She believed in me and was proud to be in my presence. At such a low point in my life, that was an invaluable gift. I don't know how—or even if—I would have gotten through rehab without Tina. In addition to her "angelic" gifts—I don't want you to get the idea that she was some kind of fallen saint, because she wasn't—what made her so special was that she was completely human. She had a wild, if not wicked, sense of humor, amazing optimism, and charisma. I liked to think that Tina was a part of me that I had forgotten I possessed. You would think that being around this fabulous woman would bring on the breakthrough aha moment, wouldn't you? Well, actually, it didn't. It wasn't until a big, hard-core, mean- and scary-looking ex-con checked into the place that my aha moment really came. Tina helped me wake up; James helped me become aware.

The first time I saw James was the night he was admitted. He was kicking a monstrous heroin habit. Before I even describe meeting him, let me just emphasize that, when you are in the midst of kicking any substance addiction, you look and feel like crap—plain and simple! Anyway, back to meeting James. There sat this mean- and-scary-looking guy outside the nurses' office, waiting to get a dose of something to help him through the initial heroin withdrawal.

He had very dark eyes and a mean, penetrating stare. The nurses' station was next to Tina's and my room, so I had to pass that area for anything and everything, including a bathroom trip. The first time I saw James, I smiled and said hi, wanting to give him a cheerful welcome. The look he gave me in return put lightning in my step; I wanted to get down the hall and away from him as fast as possible. His eyes bore right through me. Without his saying a word, I could tell he was thinking, *Shut up, little girl, before I knock that smile right off your face.* I thought he might even stab and kill me on the spot. By the time I came back to the nurses' station, he was gone. I was so thankful I didn't run into him again that night.

The next morning, again, he was outside the nurses' station sitting in his tough-guy pose, with his arms crossed in such a way as to show all his tattoos. I thought, *He probably had a rough day yesterday. I'll just give him a nice welcoming smile to help him feel more comfortable, but I won't say anything.* So, I smiled and nodded to him as I walked past, even though, as I walked down the hall to approach him, he had followed me with his eyes, giving me the most chilling stare I have ever seen. It really scared me, even more so than the night before. It shook me up to realize that, not only had I never come into contact with anyone like this before (I knew that, actually), but now I was going to have to live with him. That was horrifying, considering that I had already decided there was no doubt about it: He was absolutely going to stab me.

The next few times I had to pass him, I just kept my head down and made no eye contact whatsoever. I thought about getting a hand mirror to hold around the hall doorway so I could see if he was there or not. It seemed over the top, but I was more than merely uncomfortable even thinking about having to pass him. That night at bedtime, I was beyond thankful that he wasn't out there.

Having the daily schedule down by that point into my stay, I was up early and ready to head down to breakfast a couple of mornings later. I went down the hall with a lively step, feeling good—hope was returning, and I held onto it tight, just as Tina had said I should. As soon as I turned the corner from my room, there sat James, staring at me. Fear jolted all the bounce right out of me, and I thought to myself, *I'll just put my head down and walk as fast as I can until I get past him. It'll be okay.* I was about three steps away from him when I clearly heard him say, "Hello." I was the only one in the hall, so there was no mistaking that he was talking to me.

I spun around, more out of pure shock than to be polite by returning his greeting. "Hi!" I said, surprising myself with my own friendliness, given that I had been petrified seconds before. But, a split second later, my shocked surprise turned into a happy one: I realized that he was smiling at me. I did a mini-double take when I saw that smile—it was warm and open, the kind of smile you expect to see on the face of a dear friend you haven't seen in a long time. In a way, that is what James and I were to each other, on the soul level (more about that in Chapter 5). I beamed back an equally big, warm smile.

"I'll see ya," he said.

"See ya," I promised over my shoulder as I continued on to breakfast.

Suffice it to say that he completely turned all my judgments about him upside down as soon as I saw that smile. That was my aha moment—that smile from the same person I had convinced myself mere hours before was going to stab me.

> *Treat people as if they were what they ought to be, and you will*
> *help them become what they are capable of becoming.*
> **—Johann Wolfgang von Goethe**

It's Circle Time, Children

Sharing. Whether it brings up ambivalent memories of your favorite toy being destroyed by a younger sibling, or painful flashbacks of honest revelations to significant others that you imagined would lead to true intimacy but, in reality, brought only despair and isolation, the word *sharing* conjures up a heap of emotions in most of us. I guess it might bring up warm emotions in some people; among addicts, this is rarely, if ever, the case. That being said, let's just say that when we knew it was "circle time" in rehab, we didn't exactly jump for joy or delude ourselves that we were going to sit cross-legged, hold hands, and sing "Kumbaya."

Sharing in rehab meant exposing the core of oneself, which, to me, meant shame. In retrospect, I realize it probably meant exactly the same thing to everyone else there, but at the time, my awareness was not that inclusive. I wanted to get better because I wanted to move on. I guess what I should say is, I wanted to be better; I didn't want to get better. Getting better meant doing the work, and doing the work just hurt too much. But I was already understanding, at least a little bit, that the only way out is the way through.

So, through I went—with baby steps, but forward, nonetheless.

So, back to sharing. Part of rehabilitation is talking—about how you feel, what your challenges are, what you hope for, and, perhaps most important of all, what you want to release. It wasn't exactly phrased that way by the counselors, but we got the point when we were handed the Twelve Steps workbooks, attended mandatory classes, and watched scores of monotonous videos. To me, the Twelve Steps program seemed very elementary and vague; the best way I can describe it is that I felt like we were being given busy work, without receiving any real therapy that we could use on an everyday, practical basis. In other words, we were not really getting treatment that would help us heal.

Before I get into this any further, let me make it perfectly clear that I'm not knocking the setup of the program, because the Twelve Steps program has helped a lot of people over time. A great number of people were so far away from living a typical life in mainstream society that the Twelve Steps process was an easy one for them to understand and implement. It offered a step-by-step system that is very helpful and nurturing for people who are so lost that they don't know where to go or who to turn to. If that's where a person is, by all means, he or she should use the Twelve Steps program—cling to it as a lifeline, if need be. Whatever it takes to get and stay clean, do it! Kudos to everyone who does so.

Because the Twelve Steps program was what our rehab center based its program on, we always had activities that centered on our reciting from some addiction book. I think I would have been okay with that part, even at that point. What tripped me up was the next part: We had to link the passage we read to our everyday lives. *Seriously? Do you think it's a good idea to group-share what your home life was like—with a bunch of strangers?*

Maybe you are a step ahead of where I was then. Let's cut to the chase. Yes, this brought up the same reaction in me as hearing Gossip Girl dis me because of my shoes. But I don't mean that in a petty or mean-spirited way. I felt ashamed that I had so much, yet couldn't make it enough—Tina's shared wisdom about the empty place inside all of us helped, but it was not enough to heal my shame. Learning takes time, and I wasn't giving that time to myself. As a result, I continued to cycle between shame and pain and self-disgust. I hated where I was, and I hated who I was. And that self-hatred blocked my ability to heal.

At that point in my journey, this horrible forced circle time was pure torture for me in more ways than one. How could I possibly feel comfortable talking about my awful life in my awful custom-built home, driving my awful Lexus, while wearing my awful Rolex? I didn't know how to do it, or how I would ever get used to doing it, but I knew I had to do it. So I made up my mind to try.

It was another who-would-have-guessed-you-were-a-guardian-angel fellow rehab member who showed me how to do what I needed to do.

One day I was sitting in the circle next to Valerie, who launched into a share before we were even told it was time for our "official" group share.

Without so much as a second's hesitation, Valerie turned toward me. "You know what my life was like the last two years, Brienne?"

I shook my head. I had already been in rehab long enough to know that whatever I was about to hear would more likely than not make my hair stand on end, send shivers down my spine, and keep me from sleeping at night. But I also knew I had to listen; later, I came to see that my mission while in rehab, more than anything else, had been to listen to the others who had it worse than I ever had or ever would.

"I lived in a kind of camp with my boyfriend. You know the kind I mean. We're homeless. Hobos. Whatever you call us these days." She said it matter-of-factly, with no bitterness or resentment; she hardly even sounded sad. That broke my heart even more. "My boyfriend beat me all the time. He raped me once, too." She added the last part almost as an afterthought, but again, without even a trace of anger, bitterness, or grief. She just accepted that what was, was.

As she told me this story, I mentally replayed another one that she had told previously, about how she and her mother liked to share meth and drink a six-pack for breakfast. *How could she not wind up using? She has an understandable excuse.* Tina's words echoed, but I had to struggle to hear them. I guess it's true that a lot of people with problems as bad as Valerie's—and, horrifyingly, even worse than hers—don't ever use or become addicts, so it stood to reason that she did what she did because it was the best she could do. If that was true, then it also stood to reason that, quite simply, I, too, had done the best I could do at the time. And helping myself heal and move on with my life was the best I could do now, just as Tina always said.

In the midst of this stream of thought, Valerie brought me up short. Of all the things she had said up to that moment, the most horrifying and shocking of all was this: "Guess how old I am, Brienne?" she grinned, knowing I wouldn't possibly give the correct answer. To save me from mortifying myself, she answered her own question herself. "I'm thirty-seven."

That did it. More than anything else, that grounded me to the earth, to reality. She was only two years older than I was, yet it easily looked like a twenty-year age difference. The loss of her teeth, the permanent tweak behavior of rocking and fidgeting, the deep crevasses of wrinkles, the aged and weathered skin, and the hunched-over, worn-out body made it next to impossible to look at the two of us and consider us comparable, age-wise.

From the moment I started listening to Valerie—not just hearing her stories, but really listening to what she had to say—my perspective on people changed permanently. It was through her that I realized how much of an effect quality of life could have on a person. Life had dealt her one of the worst hands of cards I could ever imagine. But her stories did not stick in my mind merely because of how disturbing they were; they stuck in my mind because I watched her move through life in a way that showed that her spirit could not be broken. No matter how much physical and emotional abuse her body, heart, and mind sustained, she persevered. That is spirit. That is soul. She recounted a horrendous childhood—compounded by her adult life with her brutal boyfriend—yet never once did I hear her place blame or show anger. I felt that, although she had endured many hardships, she never lost her smile or her positive view. Without her saying this to me in so many words, I came to intuitively understand that faith (she might not have called it that) led her to accept that this was the life she was here to carry out, and that this was the life she had chosen in order to learn what she needed to so that she could become a better person. The person she was destined to be in this lifetime, so her soul could move on.

Before I understood all this on an intuitive level, though, I will honestly tell you that I was dumbfounded to observe her laughter, smile, hugs, and optimism. Every trivial complaint I had ever made or heard was echoing and ringing in my ears. This was a lesson to be learned: I was watching a strong woman take the cruel lot she'd been given in life, which some might judge to have been no better than a pile of garbage, and turn it into a gleaming diamond of her own.

I have never felt more like a pile of trash for all the shallow, meaningless, negative thoughts I endured—both what I thought of others without necessarily getting to know them, and what I sensed others thought of me. All these years, I had spent time and energy caring about absolutely nothing, all the while taking everything that mattered for granted. By this I mean that, for the most part, negative thoughts are not about anything that is really significant. Without being fully aware of it at the time, I was able to think back and pick out those who were there throughout my life up to that point, and those who were not, in terms of deep and meaningful connection. It is a hard concept to accept, regardless of whether we understand it or not—but, as I accepted it, I began to see that we are all here on this earth for a very specific reason.

Make the most of yourself for that is all there is of you.
—**Ralph Waldo Emerson**

The Wild Kingdom—Not Just of Animals

Everything on God's green earth has its place and its purpose, and we humans delude ourselves into thinking we are more significant than any other living thing. To make matters worse, we delude ourselves even further by thinking that some people are more significant than other people. By more significant, I mean more important, more deserving, more worthwhile—for whatever reason. The truth is, no one person is better than another. More money, more brains, better looks are all too often equated with better personhood, when nothing could be further from the truth. However, what is also true is that some people behave better than others. More often than not, the ones you might expect to behave badly turn out to be gems, and the ones who seem to shine on the outside are rotten to the core. Most of us have to figure out who's who and what's what the hard way. Life is a wild kingdom, in more ways than one. But all the wild things are not animals. A wild thing might be fierce in order to protect itself, but that does not mean it can't also be gentle and beautiful. Some of the best people I've ever known—and ever will know—were as rough as could be on the outside, but on the inside, they were soft and warm and tender. And their kindness and love still light my way.

In rehab, there was a certain camaraderie among those who had served real time in life, whether in jail or out on the streets. That was certainly a club I felt excluded from, and uncomfortable in the midst of, so I often sat back and did a lot of silent observation. This particular part of rehab taught me that you can learn a lot by keeping your mouth shut. The more I observed without commenting, the more I noticed that there was a definite yet invisible line between those who had been "roughed up" by life and those who had not been.

As the cliques formed and people settled into them, I began to notice something very odd. It seemed that the really roughed-up ones—whom I had come to collectively think of as the "elders" because of their life experience, not their chronological ages—wanted to protect me from life by constantly giving advice about what not to do. When a new recruit came in and began to wax poetic about the "wonders" of drugs—including where to get them locally—the elders quickly shut them up, informing them that I was a "good girl" and that they had better not "ruin my ears."

As in, they'd better not tell me poisonous lies that I might believe, given my status as a relatively novice user, thereby destroying my chances to break free of the vicious cycle of addiction. Even then, I could feel that it was as if they projected themselves onto me, trying to save me from their own harsh fate—because they couldn't save themselves. In hindsight, I'm certain this is exactly what they were doing. And they did save me, each and every blessed one of them.

Intuitively, I trusted what they were doing and followed their lead. But I couldn't help but want to know more about their lives. It was intriguing to hear their stories, to learn about the kinds of lives I would never have even glimpsed pre-rehab. It wasn't that I was thinking about using again; I was just enthralled by these lives that I could not have so much as imagined before. It was a mixture of fascination and horror, but I couldn't help wanting to know.

As the saying goes, however, "nothing doing." The more I asked to hear the elders' stories, the more vigilantly they replied, "That's nothing for you to hear 'bout, Brienne." They each said this in pretty much the same words, to the point where I wondered if they had discussed it among themselves and come up with a standard answer. More likely, they just had such a common set of experiences that they sought to protect me as a way to protect the vulnerable part of themselves that no one else ever had protected . . . that they themselves had not protected.

Of all of them, James was the one who tried the hardest to drive this point deep into my consciousness. We sat talking, and, as usual, I tried to get him to share his stories with me. He turned toward me. For a long moment, he just looked at me with those penetrating eyes. The intensity of his voice matched that of his gaze when he said, "I don't ever want to see you out there, Brienne. Don't do it. Don't make me see you out there."

Our eyes locked, and I nodded. I didn't respond in words, though. I didn't need to. I understood that if I went out there and used, I wouldn't just be letting myself down, I would be letting James and all the other elders down, too.

What they meant, without saying it in so many words, was that I didn't have to succumb the way they had, because I had an opportunity to avoid that lifestyle. They saw themselves as caught in the web of fate: They could not avoid what I could. To put it another way, they had secretly voted me off their island. Protective, wise, and heartbreakingly sad, their "vote" was a warning to heed their hard-edged counsel and learn from it. So I did.

I trusted their advice for another reason, though, and a very practical one. What a drug dealer or addict believes about drugs can often turn out to be quite different from what one might assume. Over time, as I paid close attention to the elders, I observed, time and time again, that these veteran drug users adamantly issued advice to stay clear of drugs. Prior to rehab, I had always made the assumption that most addicts would preach about all the grand and amazing benefits one could have while high. In rehab, only the new admittees did this, and, as I said, the elders shut them down before they had a chance to get started—at least with me. At my point in the process at that time, it would have been easier for me to accept addicts' praising of the stuff, as opposed to listening to them detail how destructive drugs could be. But, of course, that was not the point of rehab. Healing does not entail reinforcing whatever it was that brought you to the point of needing to be healed. Healing is cleansing yourself of the poison—whatever it might be: person, behavior, or substance—so that you can re-create yourself and your life.

Let me give an example of how these discussions actually went down in rehab. I was the only person checked in at that time for singular use of powder cocaine (remember, everyone thinks coke went out with the eighties). Part of rehab involves splitting people into groups based on their drug(s) of choice (DOC). Some, like me, had a singular DOC; others, multiple substances. During the first group share that I attended, I was asked what my DOC was. When I replied, "Cocaine," the immediate collective response was, "Do you smoke it, bang it, or both?"

I had no idea you could smoke it. Naive as I was, I then found out that, when smoked, it is generally referred to as "crack." Yes, I was clueless, even though I was a user. I also had no idea that "banging it" means that the user liquefies the cocaine and then shoots it by hypodermic needle into the body. Probably the most horrifying aspect of that practice is that most who bang it use their necks as a good needle entry point. I could not even imagine someone shooting drugs into his or her neck—with a needle! I was beyond overwhelmed at how hard-core this sounded to me. At what point do you think, *Maybe I'll try sticking this needle in my neck to see what happens—see if I get a more intense high.* I mean, really, how could someone think this was acceptable to do? Then again, it's probably not any more reasonable than my thinking it was acceptable to snort cocaine at a mommies group. A big part of rehab was getting each of us to see that addiction is just not acceptable, that it is completely outside of what is acceptable. It can't be comprehended within normative thinking processes because it is a parallel mode of behavior—just as addiction is a parallel universe. That's not an excuse or a justification; it's just an explanation of how the addict's mind-set functions. Addicts become addicted because they are missing the component—the enough switch or whatever you want to call it—that tells nonaddicts, without their even needing to think about it, that what they are contemplating taking/doing is not acceptable behavior.

There I go, digressing again. Back to the actual share sessions. In addition to my shock as a result of exposure to hard-core cocaine techniques was the reality that, to my fellow rehab mates, I was not a hard-core user, at least not technically speaking. Eighty percent of my fellow rehab mates were heroin addicts, and the remaining percentage was a mix of meth tweakers and alcoholics. This made their responses to my powder-cocaine DOC pretty incredible—and by that I mean beyond any sort of sensible, sound logic. I received frequent lectures from them as to how "unhealthy and bad" it was to snort cocaine.

Oh, really? I thought to myself at the time. *I must have missed the news report on the health benefits of smoking meth and mainlining heroin.* I understand now that when you're in the spotlight for doing what society views as unacceptable—and all of us in rehab were in that spotlight—it's natural to try to step out of the unrelenting glare, even if it means pushing someone else into it. At the time, however, I did not appreciate it one bit. I would recall how often Steve, my personal drug dealer, would lecture about how "bad, unhealthy, and destructive" hard drugs are on the human body. Not that he ever thought twice about making a hefty income from selling cocaine. That is because Steve *sells* drugs, but he does not use drugs himself. He's actually something of a health nut; he works out and follows a health regime (including detox juice fasts), all while reaping the monetary benefits of dealing drugs. I actually met him at his gym to transact deals on more than one occasion. Even while I was using, it all struck me as damn ironic—and as I look back on it, I also see it as heartbreakingly sad. I only wish I had seen it for all it was at the time.

It is not an oversimplification to say, without qualification, that all drugs are "bad, unhealthy, and destructive" substances. Period. I should not have been outraged by how cocaine was categorized any more than I should have focused on the irony of meeting my drug dealer at his gym. At the point in the process where I was during rehab, however, I didn't have enough wisdom or clarity—or self-love—to see it that way. Thank goodness for the elders, my guardian angels, and the other guides

I encountered later on in my journey. Without them, I might never have found my way back to what matters—and to the person I was meant to become.

> *Turn your face to the sun, and the shadows fall behind you.*
> **—Maori Proverb**

Open-Mic Night

Can you hear me? Can you *really* hear me? Even if you can, are you listening—*really* listening?

We all listen best when our mouths are shut. That was a lesson I learned in rehab that has nothing to do with addiction. We all spend so much time and energy wanting to be heard that we don't listen to one another. Even worse, we don't listen to ourselves. We hear with our ears, but not with our hearts.

You hear plenty at open-mic night, rehab style. So much so that you try to shut your ears—and your heart—but the universe has a way of forcing you to hear what you need to. Eventually, you listen, because you don't have a choice.

For some people, rehab was a place where they could talk and have somebody listen. Perhaps it was the only place where anyone ever had listened. But, for me, it felt like I was sentenced to sit through the world's worst and longest open-mic night. Part of the torture was that I was too scared to talk. I guess that was the same reason why all my rehab mates felt that they could come and talk to me—or just talk *at* me, in some cases.

In-patient rehab, typically, is a melting pot of racial and cultural backgrounds that converge because of a single common denominator: drug addiction. That being the case, it is not difficult to guess that the amount of "drug talk," in and out of official group sharing, is pretty significant. It's actually around 90 percent. It is, after all, the reason for being in rehab. Nevertheless, I reached the point where I was so tired of the constant dope talk that I seriously questioned how this program was ever going to work for me. For the most part, this dope talk was always the same—the details changed somewhat from person to person, but the plot never varied; nor did the theme. Each story I heard quietly implied that drug addiction was a like an abusive love affair: The "lover" could never, and would never, want to walk away from the "beloved."

At the beginning, apart from my fascination with the stories of the elders, I tuned the rest of it out. *Love affair? I don't think so.* I just wanted to have enough energy to chase after my twins and not look like a hag when my husband got home from work. I wasn't an addict like they were addicts. I shut out their words because I couldn't identify—or, at least, I convinced myself that I couldn't; I certainly didn't want to identify or be associated with what was happening. In spite of my not wanting to identify, or maybe because of it, I became a very good listener. I took copious mental notes and eavesdropped on the conversations I was not a part of. As I said earlier, it *was* fascinating: I had never been exposed to this kind of life, and it was mind-boggling, astonishing beyond my wildest imaginings. Most important, although I was not aware of it at the time, all these observations would later become thought provoking, leading me to gain insights about who I had become, who I was now, and who I was meant to be. Again, I didn't see it at the time, but it was because I had no opportunity to get away from them that I was forced to listen to what I didn't want to hear. And I thank God for that now.

My prior community and group of close friends—my intimates, you could say—had always shielded themselves from unpleasantness in all its forms. This group, including my husband and me, did whatever it took to live in a bubble of tranquility, while avoiding harsh reality at all costs. There are not many country clubbers serving soup at the mission unless they are wearing a special ankle bracelet as a result of being oblivious to tax laws. There are always exceptions, of course, and hats off to every person from every walk of life who tries to walk in another's shoes for a while—who tries to pay it forward instead of trying to get paid back. But these special people are few and far between, indeed. The longer I lived *la dolce vita,* the clearer it became to me that the superficial was all that mattered to the people in my set. I guess you could say that the smoother one becomes, the more important it is to never get any wrinkles—or at least to see to it that no one sees the ones you have.

Even before my forced cohabitation with "the others"—elders and so on—it continually amazed me that people could be so uncomfortable when they came face-to-face with their own fears or with society's fears. Looking at the nameless, faceless "other" eye to eye can shake you to the core. We all fear losing our home. We all fear not being able to make enough money to be in the "right" crowd. We all fear not fitting in. We all fear gossip and judgment from others. But, no matter how much we fear all that, what we each fear the most is having to look at ourselves.

Some people believe that writing a check will validate their efforts to save the world. Sure it's easy to write a check, if you have the funds; but it's next to impossible to recognize a real human being—whether you have money or not. Don't get me wrong; true charity is certainly a wonderful gesture of caring by means of financial assistance from those who have more to those who have less. Too often, though, money is donated for all the wrong reasons—whether to impress others in one's set or to appear to be a better person, mistakenly believing that the mere act of donating is a requirement of being "polished," or, beyond that, proof of being polished. In truth, donating money is neither a requirement nor proof of being polished; if done from the heart, it is an act of generosity, and if done for any other reason, it is simply writing a check. No more, no less.

I have witnessed firsthand that some of the roughest rocks you could ever imagine were the most polished gems you would ever want to know. Conversely, some of the gems that sparkled brightest were really sharp-edged stones you would never want to get anywhere near if you really knew what they were made of. I am not proud of every step I made along the path that got me to reach that conclusion, but I am proud that I reached it. Prouder still to honor those who helped me get there. And I'd say it out loud at any open-mic night in the world.

Even if you're on the right track, you'll get run over if you just sit there.

—Will Rogers

4

Major Learning Curve

School—I Mean Life—Is in Session

First, you have to be awake. Next, you have to be aware. In order to live in harmony with the universe and your higher self, that is. Anyone can go through the motions of just existing, but that isn't really living. Somehow, I think addicts know this—even if they don't go about acknowledging it in a way that is good for them. By that I mean that you don't seek to numb out unless you feel deeply; you don't find the empty places excruciating if you don't feel deeply. What you long for is not unbearable unless you feel deeply. And that is why addicts numb out.

My own experiences with addiction initially seemed different than those of my rehab mates, but I came to see that they only *seemed* different to me because of what I couldn't face about myself at the time. In reality, they were not so very different at all. We all have a dark side—or at least dark places—that we hide from others and ourselves. If we do that long enough, all we do is hurt ourselves, and usually others, too—the ones we love the most, especially. I convinced myself that I used only in order to be able to keep up—to do more—but it was really because I couldn't handle that I was not able to do what those around me seemed to do so easily, and that made me feel like a failure. If I had faced things and myself honestly, I would have seen that my expectations were completely out of sync with anything reasonable.

Life gives us lessons because the universe—and whatever higher power we each believe in—wants us to become all that we are meant to be, which is the same as saying that it waits for our little everyday selves to be ready to become our higher selves. If that seems too deep or too "out there" to you, think of it this way, instead: We have to learn and grow and change because we are alive, and that is what being alive means.

Because they are so intense, addiction and rehab/recovery can highlight and magnify life lessons. Take it from me: They can, and they do! Think of them as a crash course on life. Life 101, the accelerated program. Addicts who want to recover embrace this, because doing things in a slow, methodical way just doesn't resonate for us. (Slow and methodical is different from living one day at a time, but more about that later.) Right, wrong, or in between, we are what we are, each and every one of us. Sadly, not every addict recovers, but the ones who do, don't manage it by means of any easy, methodical plan. They ace the crash course or they don't, in other words. And, often, they have to go through it more than once. It's part of the hitting-bottom phenomenon.

The course of my short stay in rehab turned out to be one of the most advantageous learning experiences I'd ever had. I was immersed in Life 101, the accelerated program. Fortunately, I realized early on that I had better pay attention, because, no matter how reluctant I might be at points in the process, I was in the most important class the school-of-life curriculum offered.

True, it had been years since my college days, so I was a little slow and foggy at the beginning, as I've freely admitted. For quite a while, I felt the same way I had during college lectures that were so boring that all I could do to stay focused was count how many times the professor touched his toupee. Fortunately for me, none of the rehab counselors wore toupees, so I couldn't fall back on old habits. In spite of myself, before too long, I stopped playing the mental games that allowed me to avoid paying attention, and I actually listened. As soon as I started to listen, instead of just hear, it got interesting. It stopped being just a hum of "other people" talking about "their" problems and started being the fascinating melodies of individual human stories. The more I engaged, the more I realized that all life is a symphony, but we have to listen to appreciate it.

I know, I know. I keep waxing on and on about how much I learned from my rehab experiences. But it's true; and, besides, my story wouldn't be my story without it. What I learned could not be measured in terms of course credits; nor could I compile a list of skills to put on my résumé. How would I explain that I learned how to make a homemade tattoo gun from a staple, some mattress string, and pencil graphite? Would learning the skill of bartering and trading contraband goods be considered an accomplishment or a leisure activity? Could my list of interests include my detailed knowledge of what could be done with Sharpie pens, hairspray, hand sanitizer, and orange juice? My point in bringing all this up is that, in rehab, my daily lessons were nothing shy of shocking, as I quietly listened to stories, advice, and personal recollections of and about daily life. As a result of careful listening, I came to understand two very significant things: First, simply listening to, not just hearing, another point of view can offer a lesson well worth learning; second, people's actual experiences teach more than anything else (seriously, I couldn't make this stuff up if I tried), and that's a big part of why I wrote this book.

In short, by listening, I had become an audience member as well as an actor in the world's most memorable performance: life itself, complete with comedy, drama, action, and thriller motifs, because life includes all artistic genres and modes of expression. Not to mention the infinitely colorful characters who made up the cast, all of whom touched my life in some specific way. The only question at the end of every group share was whether the just-played "scene" would fade out or abruptly end. Regardless, it always left me wanting more.

No matter how much I ever hurt and sought to numb out because of it—and feelings of emptiness and/or failure hurt deeply—I always had wanted to live fully. What I mean is that, at some level, even if subconsciously, I wanted to live to the fullest even more than I wanted to escape feeling pain. As I came to realize that, I came to realize something else of equal importance: By observing and learning from these "others," I would discover how to live fully without trying to escape pain—even though I had failed previously. Abusing painkillers and cocaine had been a mistake—a big one—but that didn't mean I had to see myself, or my life, as a mistake. Remember the old saying: "If at first you don't succeed, try, try again."

> *What do we live for, if not to make things less difficult for each other?*
>
> **—George Eliot**

Curtain Calls

By now, I'm sure I've made it abundantly clear that recognizing our "guides" in life—be they situations, experiences, ideas, or people—can help us travel farther along our path. I cannot emphasize this enough, but, in case you're thinking that I already have, in fact, emphasized it enough, I am going to share some actual scenes from rehab. As far as I'm concerned, there is no greater stage than life itself, and I could not have invented these characters.

I leave it to you to judge for yourself.

The first "act" was performed by Douglas, whose genre of choice was whining. I could hardly stand to listen to him; not only was he depressing, he was also a broken record. After a while, it was beyond redundant—it was, in a word, annoying. Douglas never wanted to listen to any advice that was offered or to take any step toward rectifying his problems. All he wanted to do was whine.

Aside from battling addiction, Douglas was in another battle—a losing battle, I should say—regarding the property where he was living, which his parents owned. According to Douglas, his uncle was trying to meddle in the property dispute—for reasons Douglas never made clear. Even now, I'm not sure if these reasons were ever clear to Douglas himself. Nevertheless, every time it was his turn to share, Douglas would recount how he had to "work the land," and how hard it was because of all the "bad" people around him. The best I was able to piece together from these various group shares was that Douglas was clearing some property onto which he planned to move his triple-wide trailer—or he was inheriting a triple-wide trailer. First of all, let me clarify that I don't even know if there is such a thing as a triple-wide trailer (until I met Douglas, double-wide was the largest I'd ever heard of). Regardless, this was the way his shares always went. At least until the last one.

Just as he finished going through the same old details of the triple-wide saga—and just as I was fighting off nodding off mid-whine—he suddenly said something different. "Yeah, so then this one day I was driving my uncle down the road to the land." Let me interject at this point to give you a visual: This is a dirt road, so imagine Douglas hanging one tanned elbow out the open window, seething in silence toward his uncle. Then all of a sudden . . .

"Wham! I felt something hard hit me in the back of the head. Whaddya think that mighta been? Nope. You'll never guess," he informed us proudly. I wondered, even at that moment, if anyone else noticed that, in his excitement as he related the story, Douglas had stopped whining. "Well, turns out, my uncle cold-cocked me with the butt of his handgun. That's right—knocked me out cold. And then he pushed me outta the truck. Yeah, right outta the pickup, while I was driving."

Douglas sat back and folded his arms across his chest as he surveyed our reactions to his revelation. *That* redefines road rage, for sure. I didn't know what to say.

"Then what happened?" Gossip Girl wanted to know.

"I woke up—y'know, much later. In the dirt." The whine crept back into his voice as soon as he had to answer the question. I guess once the drama was stolen from him, it was no longer exciting to tell the story.

"I meant, what happened to your uncle?" Gossip Girl rolled her eyes. "And if you were knocked out cold, how do you know what he hit you with?"

"I'm telling you he hit me. He took the land. . . ." The rest of his share segued into the same old same old of the triple-wide saga. I assumed that, after knocking Douglas out, his uncle slid into the driver's seat and sped down the dirt road to claim triple-wide paradise. How he eluded the authorities after assaulting Douglas was never explained, nor were any other details of the outcome. Maybe everyone else picked up on the same thing I did after Gossip Girl interjected: The actual events did not matter to Douglas; the truth, for him, was that he had been irrevocably wronged. And there was just no way he could ever be compensated.

I came to see that this is true for most of us. If you can't move beyond a wrong, the details don't matter. All that matters is your own hurt; you nurse it for so long that it takes on a life and a force of its own—you may not even remember the truth of the details after a while. These hurts are the very ones that we *must* let go of, and the details don't matter. Even if we were wronged, it is more important to let go so we can move on than it is to get the other person to admit how much they hurt us—to acknowledge how wrong they were to wrong us. If you have to work that hard to get the admission from the other person, it probably isn't worth having. Even if you do get that admission—which most of us don't—it probably won't mean as much as you think it will . . . and you'll wonder only, "Is this what I waited for all these years? *That's it?!*" If Douglas had let it go, he might never have become an addict in the first place.

If Douglas was the resident whiner, Big John was the resident strong-and-silent type—a gentle giant. Getting Big John to talk—at group share and otherwise—was like pulling teeth. Again, you need a visual. Big John weighed about 350 pounds and was well over six feet tall. To me, that made him a giant. In addition to being quiet to the point of silence, he was also extremely polite, and he seemed to enjoy helping the staff by lifting heavy boxes and moving furniture when it was time to set up for our group meetings.

Now that you have an image of Big John, enter Maryanne, a bona fide alcoholic and tweaker in her mid-fifties. On top of all that, Maryanne was also what can be described only as a nut job. I say that in a nonjudgmental way; being in recovery does not make a person a nut job, nor does having mental-health issues that require counseling and treatment. Maryanne was a nut job because she avoided getting the kind of assistance that would really help her heal. At least, that is my humble opinion as her rehab mate.

To continue the visual, Maryanne wore a wig because, when she tweaked, she would often pull her hair out.

One day at outdoor recreation time (we were allowed a half hour every day to go outside), Maryanne and Big John were tossing a football back and forth. Make sure you have the visual: A bewigged, nutty tweaker and a near-silent giant playing football. I sat on a bench, serene and content as I soaked up some of the afternoon's warm sunshine. I was watching these two only peripherally; it was an amusing sight, but not worth paying close attention to. Until the next moment, that is. I do not say that to be overly dramatic, but what happened next was horrifying and disturbing—yet hilarious.

"Go deep, Maryanne!" Big John called out. He played football with some of the other guys on occasion, and these calls constituted the majority of his spoken words. In any case, he tossed the football to Maryanne in such a way that she had to jump up in order to catch it.

Here comes the horrifying-and-disturbing-yet-hilarious part, which no one possibly could have anticipated: As Maryanne jumped to catch the pass, her wig went flying off. As he saw the wig take flight, strong-and-silent Big John let out a scream. Let me emphasize that this was not the yell one might expect from a man his size; it was the high-pitched shriek of a schoolgirl. I don't know which was worse: seeing Maryanne without her wig, or hearing a 350-pound giant scream like a girl.

Meanwhile, Maryanne, from whom any of us would have expected that shriek to emanate, did no more than let out an audible gasp, her body twisting as she struggled to catch the ball and reclaim the airborne wig. She missed both, but not for lack of trying. (Her skills as a contortionist were pretty impressive, I might add.) Let's just say that Maryanne gave new meaning to the phrase, "Go deep."

To make things worse, Maryanne took an eternity to put the thing back on—clearly, a mirror was needed to complete this process effectively. All the while, Big John paced around, pretending nothing had happened—neither the wig flight nor his own shriek in response. As for me, it took every ounce of my strength to keep my laughter from erupting in guffaws.

A minute or so later, the whistle blew to let us know it was time to go back in for lineup, which saved us all. Still sitting on the bench, trying to contain myself, I watched Maryanne head back toward the building.

Big John walked directly over to me as I stood up to collect my stuff from the bench and go inside. Stopping dead in his tracks, he looked me straight in the eye. In a voice completely devoid of emotion, he said, "That . . . was . . . awful." He looked as if he had just seen a ghost or witnessed something else that had scared the life out of him. Before I could answer, he turned and went inside.

I followed him in silence, still struggling to contain my laughter. Even now, I chuckle every time I think of that huge dude emitting such a girlie shriek. I know Maryanne must have been mortified, but if she looked back on it now, I hope she'd see the humor. Then again, maybe not. Sometimes our sense of humor is all that keeps us going—all that keeps us sane. If Maryanne had a sense of humor, she probably wouldn't have been such a nut job.

> *He who laughs, lasts.*
>
> **—Mary Pettibone Poole**

Family Affair

One day at a time. This is a key tenet of Twelve Steps. One that is deceptively simple. Taking things one step at a time helps us focus on the process, rather than the outcome. It is our outcome-oriented society that often makes us feel overwhelmed, so learning how to do this helps us overcome addiction and move forward in true recovery.

It is also important to understand that the one-day-at-a-time, one-step-at-a-time philosophies are extremely helpful to addicts because addicts live in the moment. This is the place where addictive behavior seems reasonable or acceptable—the place where we convince ourselves that one more drink or one more snort or one more line is all we need . . . that we'll give it up "later." Not just that we will or that we even can, but that we'll want to. Which, in reality, is pretty unlikely. Nevertheless, in the moment of convincing ourselves, we truly do believe the lie. And that is what trips us up, time and time again, until we get to the point that we're really and honestly ready to do the work it takes to recover and heal.

Part of getting to that point is accepting that we can't change the part of ourselves that is encoded to live in the moment; spontaneous, fly-by-the-seat-of-their-pants people cannot suddenly become cautious. What we can do is learn how to use the best parts of ourselves to help make the most troublesome parts better; to accept that we are what we are, but that we don't have to keep hurting ourselves. That is the best and the most anyone can do, addicts and nonaddicts alike—accept the little everyday self in order to become the higher self.

Eventually it stops feeling like work and starts feeling like life, but it is a perpetual process. Like any process, some parts are hard, some parts are boring, and other parts are fun and wonderful. The key is to let ourselves just be where we are and not judge where we are for what "it" is, but, rather, just accept that we are where we need to be—and everything changes, cycling between good and bad, just as the universe intends.

Once we each accept that, living gets easier, because we understand that we are just travelers, and the peaks and valleys are not there to specifically daunt us or harm us in any way. We coast; we climb; we coast again. One step at a time, one moment at a time, one day at a time.

I promised that this was not going to be too New Age-y a book, so before you get the idea that I'm going to start saying "om" in the middle of every section, let me bring the story back to the nitty-gritty of rehab. I am about to introduce you to two of the most unforgettable characters I met there: Joanie and Janie. If you're thinking they sound like twins from a sixties sitcom, you're not too far off; Joanie and Janie were two older women who were, in fact, blood relatives (cousins, to be exact), but not twins. None of that is what made them unforgettable. What made them unforgettable is that they truly were real-life examples of what it means to live life one day at a time—and take things one step at a time.

Let me show you what I mean. Before I do, though, I need to back up for just one more second to explain another aspect of rehab: the ever-changing community (or "cast," depending upon how you think about your rehab mates!). When you stay in an in-patient rehab program, you tend to see a lot of people come and go for various reasons. Some people graduate; some get kicked out; and some just disappear into the night, never to be heard from again. As a result, new people constantly come in to quickly fill up the vacated spots. During my second week in rehab, the first of the two cousins, Joanie, arrived.

Joanie was a little white-haired grandma (seventy-two years old, by her own admission), sporting a little grandma denim shirt with embroidered stars, tennis shoes with ribbons for laces, and cute capri pants. She introduced herself and her five-year addiction to meth and then proceeded to make herself comfortably at home.

Excuse me? Did I hear correctly? How in the world does a seventy-two-year-old, decently put-together woman develop a five-year-long meth habit?

I must not have done a good job masking my shock, because, without missing a beat, Joanie said, "Yes, dear, that's right. Meth." She gave me a warm smile—lips closed, lest she reveal signs of meth mouth, no doubt—and sat back serenely.

I assure you that it was completely freaky to hear an admission of a five-year meth addiction from someone who looked like the strongest stuff she ever put in her body was hot chocolate. This was a woman who should be knitting afghans and tucking her grandkids into bed with a goodnight story after warm milk and cookies. Suppressing the urge to shake my head in utter bewilderment, I just sat quietly. I was already learning that we each had a different story to tell, but the one part of every story that was always the same was this: We each took a wrong turn somewhere along the line.

"I'm sure you're all wondering how a nice little old lady like me took up a meth habit," Joanie said lightly, in keeping with her grandmotherly charm. Here she was, the newest among us, and she was trying to make *us* feel comfortable. She took a deep breath before continuing. "It was because of my daughter. She's been a user for years." The smile had vanished, but you could see her love for this substance-addicted adult daughter shining in her eyes. "Anyway, she was headed off to jail and gave me her purse for safekeeping. There was a packet of meth hidden in it that the police hadn't found . . . and I . . . well, I thought that if I tried it, maybe I would be able to understand how she felt. Why she did it. Something that would help me help her. Lord knows I had tried everything else."

The love was still shining in her eyes, despite her sadness. She didn't say anything else for a bit, but her pain was palpable. This woman loved her daughter so much that she risked what trying the drug might do to her in order to see why it had so captivated her daughter. Maybe she just wanted to stare into the face of the enemy that was destroying the person she loved the most, hoping that if she did so, she would be able to destroy it. But, unfortunately, as is all too often the case, no such luck.

"One try and I was hooked." Joanie confirmed what we already knew about her—and ourselves. "That stuff gave me more energy than I'd had in years!" I caught her eye and nodded—I knew all too well exactly what she meant and how she felt. She leaned over and patted my knee in tacit understanding. "Plus, my arthritis didn't hurt anymore. I just felt better than I had in decades. Maybe than I ever had. I didn't want to ever stop feeling that good. . . ." Her voice trailed off at the last part, as she looked around the circle and saw that we all knew, because we all had been there. The details of why addicts get hooked may differ from person to person, even if it all stems from the inability to fill that emptiness inside; regardless, being held in the thrall of the addiction is the same. We think it's different for each of us; we feel special to our "beloved," but we're not. Only once we see and accept that can we move past it.

As she sat there scanning our faces, this little white-haired lady seemed to intuitively get this—maybe because she had experienced it not just as an addict herself, but as the mom of an addict. Or maybe she had just made up her mind, prior to checking herself into treatment to kick her hard-core meth addiction, that she was going to successfully recover.

As I pondered all these possibilities, Joanie, in a gentle yet firm voice, set the record straight. "This isn't my first time in rehab, but it is going to be my last. I am going to get through it this time, and so are all of you." I guess you could call it talking the talk and walking the walk, granny style. Before the next person started to speak, Joanie added, "We're all in the same boat. We'll just have to help each other get through it, won't we? This, too, shall soon pass."

Yes, it shall. And it does. Without Joanie, it might not have for the rest of us.

Before the next meeting rolled around, another older lady was admitted. We all had tacitly adopted Joanie as our rehab grandma, and this newbie would not give her any competition for that title. The new arrival could best be described as a *glam*ma, not a grandma. I happened to be near the admitting area when she arrived and was surprised to see how glammed up she was, given her age. Dressed to the nines, she wore lots of gold and diamond jewelry and had a great tan and perfect hair and makeup.

"Hi! I'm Janie," she said to me, extending a slender, bronzed arm to shake my hand. The diamonds caught the light and sparkled as her arm bounced lightly when I gripped her hand in mine.

"Hi, Janie. I'm Brienne. Welcome."

"Thank you, darling. Know where I can get a very dry martini?" She gave me a sly wink and then laughed. "Joking," she assured the staff member behind the desk.

I smiled at her, and she smiled in return, showing perfect teeth between her matte-finish dark-red lips. I could hardly wait to hear her stories in group; from this brief scene, I could tell she was the standard life-of-the-party alcoholic. Nine chances out of ten, she also mixed the best dry martini you could ever have.

Janie was fun, cracked jokes, and had such a bubbly personality that you couldn't possibly not like her. Everyone was "darling" and "honey" and all sorts of other names that made us feel good. If Joanie was the grandma who read you stories and baked you cookies, Janie was the eccentric older aunt who let you stay up past your bedtime, telling you about her adventures as you yawned, wide-eyed with delight and fascination. Rehab would not have been the same without either one of them.

By the end of the second group meeting, my perception of Janie had expanded. Up to that point, I had imagined her to be the best-ever hostess, regaling her guests with funny stories—and getting them drunk on her incredible martinis—never closing the door behind the last departing guest until three in the morning . . . that is, if they were able to make it home at all. Most likely, Janie wound up passed out face-down on the bed at the end of every single one of her own parties. She was practically running the group by the end of her first session. We were all laughing and feeling more comfortable with one another than ever before; in fact, I felt that all we were missing at this "party" were drinks and hors d'oeuvres. Except that we were missing one thing at that first meeting Janie attended: Joanie. (I guess she must have not been feeling well, because attendance at group was mandatory, otherwise.)

No one really thought much about it until the next meeting, which was Janie's second. A few of us were already there when Janie arrived. Next thing we knew, in walked Joanie, who looked straight at Janie, threw her arms up in the air and exclaimed, "Well, oh-my-Goddamn, Janie, look at you here!"

The two of them squealed in delight like high-school cheerleaders. Then they hugged each other as if they were best friends who hadn't seen each other in years.

That's when it really got interesting. I already told you that they were cousins, but that meeting greeting was where we all first found out. In addition, I didn't already tell you that it turned out that Janie and Joanie already had been through rehab together. (We later learned that Janie had been in rehab more times than Joanie had.)

Neither Joanie nor Janie knew the other was checked in this time, because they hadn't been in touch for a while. They more than made up for lost time, though. It was as if they had never gone longer than a day without seeing or speaking to each other throughout their lives. They knew each other's addiction histories and finished each other's sentences most of the time. Outside of group, they would sit together, swapping stories and catching up on family news.

During one particular group meeting, Janie was going on about how she had been a closet alcoholic for years, yet successfully hid it from her family. "I could get an Academy Award for the acting I've done!" was the way she put it.

"Don't clear off the mantel just yet, dear," Joanie retorted. "You weren't quite as good an actress as you thought you were." Joanie paused and then added, "Remember, I was sober then."

"Well, she was sober, that's true." Janie beamed a smile, turning her head to include all of us in the circle. "But I think she just doesn't appreciate my talent."

The rest of us laughed.

"Mm-hmm." Joanie joined in the laughter. "Do you want to tell them, or should I?"

"What? When did I not fool everyone? Are you talking about my falling in the pool with my glass still in my hand? Or my knocking Donnie's wig off?" Janie demanded, with a straight face and a tone so serious, I wondered if those were isolated occurrences or par for the course at their family gatherings. Actually, compared to most of the family affairs I already had heard about, this was pretty tame stuff. The love that was between them, in spite of and because of all they'd been through together, was what helped us all see the humor in it. (Although, at "knocking Donnie's wig off," Big John turned white, and Maryanne held her breath.)

"We'll have to have a family reunion when we both get out of here," Janie said to Joanie, who agreed. "Mocktails for me and anti-inflammatories for you," she continued firmly. "Hell! I can still jump in the pool with my glass in my hand and all my clothes on."

"Maybe *I'll* knock off that damn wig!" Joanie whooped.

We all laughed—even Big John. (Maryanne didn't laugh, but she did keep breathing.)

In a nutshell, that was Joanie and Janie. All I can say further about them is that, if responding to your problems with that much good humor—and that much love—isn't taking things one step at a time and living life one day at a time, then I don't know what is.

> *Happiness comes of the ability to feel deeply, to enjoy simply, to think freely, to risk life, to be needed.*
>
> **—Storm Jameson**

5

Soul Trip

Synchronicity—Why Truth Is Stranger than Fiction
Truth is definitely stranger than fiction, more often than not. Most of us have experienced this to be the case, without necessarily knowing the reason why. It's a little something called *synchronicity*. This term describes the coincidence of events that might seem related but that were not caused by one another—or, at least, that cannot be explained in terms of standard cause and effect. Most often, the term is used in psychology by proponents of Carl Jung.

For the rest of us, synchronicity validates such popular phrases as "Nothing is ever random"; "Everything happens for a reason"; and "That is some crazy stuff right there!" The last phrase was the one used as an example by the person who introduced me to synchronicity: James, the hard-core ex-con (more about that in a bit).

Although I came to appreciate synchronicity even more as I traveled farther along my path—and I continue to do so—even at that point, when my awareness was only just beginning, I was intrigued. Once your consciousness is awakened—once you open to the universe—lessons and guides present themselves. We are usually more ready than we think we are, and the universe, knowing this even though we do not yet know it, sends us what we need.

Rehab is a kind of crucible. Elements are mixed into it, but in order for the wisdom of its lessons to gel, a little fire is necessary. Awareness is a form of fire—in the figurative sense. Other crucial, life-defining moments can serve as crucibles, too. The point is, we find ourselves at the crossroads throughout our lives; one moment can change our lives forever. More often than not, we don't see these moments coming, even if we look for them. That doesn't mean we are not aware, just that we needed the lesson . . . and the universe is smarter than we are. However, being aware does mean that, when those life-defining moments occur, we make the most of them—even if we have to do so after the fact.

Synchronicity is all this and more. It's like telling yourself, "Don't be scared of the weird stuff; just be. What's right for you will find you, and when it does, if you are open to it, you'll become *you*." Here's how it happened for me.

Yes, strangely enough it was James who first steered me toward my spiritual journey. The hard-core ex-con who I'd convinced myself was planning my murder turned out to be one of the most incredible human beings I've ever known. If he sounds like a most unlikely guardian angel, you'll probably think he was an equally unlikely spiritual mentor and guide. When I first met him, I would have agreed with you. We would have been wrong on all counts. Remember, guides and angels don't usually look like what we're conditioned to expect.

A short time into rehab, I realized that I had initially mistaken the penetrating quality of James's eyes for meanness. In reality, he just related to the world, and everything and everyone, with an intensity that made most people uncomfortable. That kind of intensity is something addicts have to learn how to deal with. We tend to either try to heighten it or numb it out, but it's a part of ourselves that we just need to accept and make peace with. Intensity makes life both incredibly beautiful and desperately painful—and that's just the way it is. Recovery means reconciling the dark and light parts of ourselves, and then moving through life as a whole person. It's difficult to be creative or innovative without the spark and enthusiasm that are part of intensity. Learning about synchronicity helped me realize that later on.

But back to James. Once I got over my initial fear and realized that he had not ever wanted to kill me, he and I became friends. Good friends, eventually. As I said earlier, I believe that he and I were friends before we actually met; soul friends on the same journey, just waiting for the moment when our paths would cross and we could meet. James believed that, too, although, from appearances alone, we were quite an odd pair.

I was someone who never had a brush with the law, followed what I was told, went through school, and had a definite schedule for the next sixty years of my life. He was an ex-con and a rebel, had no family to speak of, and was uneducated. (I don't think he finished high school, but I could be wrong; we never talked about it.) To clarify, he was an ex-con: He had been in jail *and* spent time in prison (in that world, jail and prison are not synonymous; prison is worse). At one time, he had been homeless, but at the time he checked into rehab, he was running a very successful drug ring. (We never discussed the details; that was also, "Not something for you to hear 'bout, Brienne. Don't make me see you out there. You remember what I said.")

Let me clarify that when I describe James as "uneducated," I am referring to his lack of schooling. This guy had more street smarts and life experience than most people twice his age. Chronologically he was only thirty; but, in terms of wisdom and experience, he was at least twice that.

Although our deep spiritual connection resonated for me at that time, the pivotal, life-changing effect it was to have on me was one I would not realize for many months. James, being James, undoubtedly recognized this, but like most wounded healers, he was more the show-don't-tell kind of teacher.

My "indoctrination" into universal wisdom and synchronicity began ordinarily enough; as I said, these things usually do. James had the words *Soul Trip* tattooed across his knuckles. This had intrigued me from pretty early on. One day, when I felt we were good-enough friends for me to ask him about it, I did.

"Hey, James. What's the ink mean?" I gestured toward his knuckles.

"Like it? Thought you might. It's the trip we're all on. I don't mean with junk." I nodded as he launched into a deep discussion—or monologue, I guess I should say—of the universe. "The universe is huge, Brienne, huge. Bigger than anything we can relate to. Bigger than outer space. And people . . . people, man, they're just clueless. Completely clueless."

"Of how insignificant they are?" I was feeling a little uncomfortable accepting my new speck self. If I were so insignificant, how come I had to work so hard? Why did any of us have to? Nothing we did really mattered.

Reading my mind, he said, "That's where you're wrong, right there. Everything matters. But it only matters together. In sync. A butterfly moves its wings, or you blow a puff of air. There's a wind current after. Miles away, it becomes a tornado. See what I mean?"

I nodded in amazement. I saw exactly, and I was captivated. Fascinated. The wonder of it burned away my doubts and fears. All I wanted was to know more. Much more. I felt as if I were hearing every worthwhile word I'd ever heard before crystallized in what James was saying now. I was understanding the universe and my place in it clearly for the first time. All I wanted was to absorb every word and learn as much as I could.

"You want to learn more? I'll tell you more." He smiled a slow smile, and the intensity of his eyes flickered and then burned. "First thing you need to understand is synchronicity. You ever hear of it?"

I shook my head; it was the first time I'd heard the term.

He explained it to me in the same way that I described it above, adding, "While I was doing time in prison, I came across this book in a pile that had been donated for us inmates. I 'randomly' picked it up, took it back to the cell, and started to read it."

"'Randomly'? You just told me nothing is random."

"Uh-huh. 'Cause nothing is. Glad you're listening to me, though. I'm telling this to you 'cause you listen so good."

He winked at me, and we smiled at each other.

"The book was called *Journey of Souls: Case Studies of Life Between Lives*. It was written by Michael Newton, PhD. I'm telling you all this so you can get yourself a copy to read. This book was my synchronicity. Might be yours, too." As James described it, the book was a catalyst for some major life-altering messages. He could not speak fast enough about what was in this book, finishing up with, "You should read it, Brienne. Read it now."

I felt I had to read the book now, too. Now, as in, *immediately*. This book recommendation was about taking the next step in my life; I knew intuitively that I *had* to read it. This was the real thing, not the superficial must-read designations of the ladies' Friday-night book club of my cupcakes-and-cocaine, pre-rehab life. This was a moment of pure synchronicity; I was certain reading the book would be, too. It was absolutely no accident or coincidence that James and I were in rehab together and that he was there to tell me about this particular book.

"Before you get the book and start reading, make sure you're ready," James said distinctly, using his "elder voice." "Reading this book is going to change your life forever, Brienne."

"I can't wait. I need to change the way I think."

He could feel my enthusiasm, how I could hardly wait for the page-by-page adventure to begin. "It's not just gonna change the way you think.

It's gonna change the way you see, and that's more important than how you think."

I nodded, still eager and fascinated, but having no real understanding about what he really meant. I couldn't possibly have understood it until I read the book myself.

"You listen to me, now." James continued his warning of what would happen after I finished the book. His elder voice held my attention, as always. "Once you start to really see things, you will *really see*. I mean, you'll see weird things, like people coming out of the woods. I'm not playing with you. And it wasn't the junk made me see it, either."

"Okay," I said meekly. I had learned to never question any of the elders.

It just so happened that my parents were scheduled to come for a visit in two days, so I immediately called them to tell them to find the book. I could hardly wait to get into something that promised to be so mysterious and powerful. James was absolutely correct in saying that it would change the way I thought and saw things forever.

Journey of Souls is a remarkable book that relates real-life encounters with the spirit world, taken from subjects under deep hypnosis. Dr. Michael Newton recorded the accounts of his patients in a study to further investigate the relationships among the spirit world, life, and death, and what these interrelationships mean. That's all I'm going to tell you about it, because if it intrigues you, synchronicity is telling you that you should read it for yourself—just as it told you to read this book for yourself.

I had never been interested in the subject before talking to James because of one reason: I already knew where I was going to end up. My Catholic upbringing had me convinced that my sins would take me directly to hell, in or out of the proverbial handbasket. Learning about synchronicity—and all the myriad wonders of the universe—taught me otherwise.

Why not go out on a limb? That's where the fruit is.
—Will Rogers

6

Mental Marathon Training

Discovering Why It's Called E*motion*

Life doesn't stand still, so neither can we, the living. We have to move through, move on, and, sometimes, simply *move*. I think that's why it's called e*motion*. Feelings come up, and then they move on. When we stay stuck, it's because at some level we want to. That can be hard to accept, but it's still true.

The sooner we accept it, the sooner we'll be able to really heal—on all levels; become who we were meant to be; and live life to the fullest. This is another way of saying that if we overlook or deny the body/mind/spirit connection, sooner or later, we will feel incomplete and/or unfulfilled.

Even if we engage with nothing else in our lifetime, we must engage with ourselves. One way or another, the universe sees to it that we each do exactly that.

I was there, right in the thick of it, so if you're thinking, *Yeah, right,* I empathize with you completely. It's exactly what I was thinking at that point in my life—the point right after I got out of rehab. That is, when I *could* think. The truth is, I was in a daze. And not unjustifiably so. In the matter of a month's time, I had been moved out of my house (remember, my ex packed me up without the Dyson), participated in an in-patient rehab program, and entered a storm of legal issues (i.e., divorce settlement). On top of all that, I had no job, and my kids were living with my ex. So, yes, I was in a daze. I will clarify that I was not in denial; I was putting into practice a lot of the insights and wisdom I'd gained in rehab, but I definitely was not "there" yet—by which I mean that I was not where I wanted to be. But I knew I was making good progress.

To put all this in perspective, it was one thing to be awake and aware in a contained environment like rehab, where, isolated from the everyday cares and duties of life, I could focus on healing. That's the purpose of in-patient treatment. Once back on the outside, however, I was on my own, without the security that rehab afforded as a safe haven. As a result, I was in a major state of confusion, uncertainty, and bewilderment. All I kept thinking to myself was, *What the* hell *did I just do?*

For me, the physical healing was not a major problem; it was the emotional aspect that was most important. Luckily, I had not traveled so far down the rabbit hole of drug abuse that I had sustained the physical indicators of abuse. Sure, I was on the pale and thin side, but as I've mentioned, I still had all my teeth (*and* a retainer).

Addressing the emotional battle ahead of me was going to be the true test. I felt as if I were entering the Iron Man competition without having ever run a mile in my life. I knew that I was going to have to make some necessary changes: physically, to a certain extent; emotionally, even more so. Even in the midst of my daze, I told myself to move on, because, the longer I waited, the worse off I would be. Rather than worry about what the future held, I focused on what I'd learned from the elders—not to mention James's recommended reading. I intuitively understood that this kind of learning was not a lesson-completed kind of thing; I was gaining awareness and wisdom as I was ready to receive it, and I trusted that it would continue to expand and evolve in its own right time. That is, the time that was best for me, and meant for me, as determined by the universe. So, it was all good, even when I felt like crap.

I had come this far already; the best I could do was just keep going, one step at a time.

> *When we do the best we can, we never know what miracle is wrought in our life or the life of another.*
> —**Helen Keller**

No Pain, No Gain

We've all heard the expression, "No pain, no gain." Sure, it's true that if you want six-pack abs, a tight butt, and firm thighs, the workouts required to attain them will be strenuous and feel less than comfortable. After all, they are *work*outs, not "*fun*outs" or "*play*outs." Physical workouts yield better bodies, and once we have attained the look we desire, we feel the work was worth the result.

Other kinds of workouts are worth the work, too—and the no-pain/no-gain principle applies to them as well. Rehab is a workout—believe me—and so is recovery. To put it another way, it is going to hurt more—a lot more—before it feels better. In case you're wondering, yes, I had to learn this the hard way, too.

Stress can take a terrible toll on the body. After I got out of rehab, the real work—or workout, if you prefer—began. I had to start facing people, addressing my own emotional issues, and signing legal papers (related to my divorce). To cut to the chase, I felt and looked like hell. I was under so much stress that my hair started falling out—rapidly. In my opinion, I looked worse at this point than I did when I was actually using drugs. My hair was thinning so fast that I ended up teasing and spraying it in order to make it appear like it had some volume. To give you a visual, when I left the house, I looked like a groupie from a Whitesnake video.

I was becoming more aware of the body/mind/spirit connection, so I knew that worrying about my stress and the toll it was taking on my body, in both visible and invisible ways, would only worsen the effects. So I decided to go proactive, instead of reactive. Exercise is an integral part of getting back into balance, physically and emotionally. That meant that I had to take exercising seriously. Which really meant that I had to take exercising seriously for the first time in my life. Yes, I would rather shop for the perfect workout outfit than actually *use* said outfit. In particular, I am not a fan of any type of cardio exercise. It would not be fair to say that I dislike the treadmill, because, in truth, I *loathe* the treadmill. I run only if I am being chased. (Remember, even when I first thought James was going to kill me, all I did was walk faster; I did not run.)

Nevertheless, I reached the point where I knew I had to start exercising. Much to my happy surprise, I discovered a good regimen that worked for me. This consisted of a cross-training combination of old-school military-style workouts (for those nonexercise types, these used to be called *calisthenics*) and meditative yoga. Some combination, huh? Before you pass judgment, remember to keep an open mind. Balance is most effective when things complement one another, working together to form a whole by each bringing out the best in the other.

As the meditative yoga began to simultaneously stimulate and relax me—physically, emotionally, and spiritually—I found that I enjoyed doing push-ups, especially when I did them outside, using whatever was around me for my equipment. I equally loved the stretching, breathing, and practicing calm that are necessary during a yoga routine. This practice taught me that being truly energized is a balance of relaxation and stimulation; when these two are combined in harmony, we feel energized. I never followed any specific routine; I just made it up as I went along. Anyone can do it. It doesn't matter if you have a state-of-the-art home gym or a pole in your bedroom, or just use water-filled milk jugs as barbells. Do whatever makes you feel good, and you will start to enjoy exercising. For those exercise haters, I was one of you! Before you start calling me a traitor, just try it a few times. Once you get into it, you'll agree with me, I'm sure. Exercise makes you feel good! [*Before you start exercising or engaging in any lifestyle-change plan, please check with your doctor or healthcare provider to make sure that you are healthy enough to begin an exercise regimen, either on your own or with a trainer. Safety and wellness come first!*]

After I started integrating exercise into my regular routine, I added another healthy habit: drinking water. I must admit that I did not do this because I wanted to; this is another positive practice that I had to learn the importance of implementing the hard way. Let me back up to explain that, whenever I am under a lot of stress, my digestive system goes haywire. I end up with the worst heartburn you could imagine. One morning I woke up with a black tongue. Yes, you read correctly: a *black* tongue! Needless to say, I completely freaked out. I was in a state of true panic, because I thought I might be dying. (It didn't help that I had watched an awful alien movie the night before.) Thoughts raced through my mind: *Sure. When I was using, nothing like this ever happened. Now that I'm clean, I have a freakin' black tongue!*

Miraculously, some glimmer of wisdom took hold of me—either from the lessons I'd been learning since rehab, the yoga, or a combination of the two. I calmed myself enough to go online and Google *black tongue*. Long story short, black tongue can be a result of acid reflux and taking too many antacids to counteract the reflux symptoms. By the time I woke up the following morning, my tongue looked normal—thank goodness. However, one instance of black tongue was enough to make me think about all the sources of stress in my life. As a result of the previous day's Google search, I had discovered that I could prevent future black-tongue moments by modifying my diet and lifestyle. One of the most important things to do was drink enough water.

Let me just say that I loathed the taste of water a little less than running on the treadmill. But everything I read confirmed the harsh reality that I, and everyone else who has not been living in a cave for the past few decades, already knew: Drinking lots of water is integral to feeling good and getting healthy. *I know!* I groaned inwardly, thinking of all the monotonous pronouncements we all have heard time and time again: "Drink lots of water!" "Drink eight glasses of water a day." Yes, everyone does need to drink a sufficient amount of water, but it does differ from person to person. And it's *not* so we continue to buy bottled water or decorative containers to carry our water around in. Simply put, human beings, like all living things, need water. We put our bodies through a tremendous amount of work every day, even while we are sleeping. Not to turn this into a biochemistry lesson, but suffice it to say that when we drink water, we are essentially replenishing the cellular structure that is slowly depleted during the course of the day.

Because water replenishes all our cells, it also plays a major role in aiding digestion. Ingesting food can either help or hinder the body. Obviously, we need nourishment in order to survive, and the quality of the food we intake plays an important part. Hence the expression, "You are what you eat." When we drink water, we are essentially flushing out the toxins we have put into our bodies. That's why black tongue can be prevented by drinking enough water.

Drinking water has many other benefits. For example, sometimes when we feel hungry, we are actually just dehydrated. In other words, our bodies send the message of "hungry" when the correct message would be "thirsty." The dehydration need is miscommunicated as pangs of, "Hungry! Must eat *now!*" Sufficient water keeps our cells properly hydrated and our fiber intake adequately balanced, which helps us feel full. In short, drinking enough water is just good for us, and it's key to being and feeling healthy.

Realistically, we are human and succumb to everyday temptations: alcohol (I'm talking about moderate consumption, not alcohol abuse/addiction); coffee (whether it's standard brew, cappuccino/latte, or coffee-based smoothies); fast food; high-calorie, high-fat snacks and desserts; and whatever else tastes great. The fact remains, though, that what goes in must come out, and water can aid with the flushing-out process. Let me emphasize that I am not touting any diet; nor am I presenting myself as having any medical or healthcare knowledge or credentials. All I am trying to do is share the benefits of my own experiences. [*As with exercise, be sure to check with your doctor or healthcare provider before embarking on any lifestyle change, including diet, nutritional supplements/vitamins/herbals, and/or increasing water intake.*]

Remember, I am not one of those born-and-bred water drinkers. Honestly, I would do anything to not have to give up my daily Diet Dr Pepper. Sigh. *C'mon. What else do you want from me? I've eliminated cocaine, painkillers, beef tacos . . . Now you want me to give up my Diet Dr Pepper?!* At first I was sad for my loss—and really sad for Dr Pepper, which had just lost a major customer. It's not like I sat around drinking an entire six-pack of the stuff every day, but it's safe to say I drank at least one a day. Now I feel great, with no more heartburn—and no more black tongue! (Soda and caffeine are two major triggers of acid reflux. Plus, sugar substitutes are not the healthiest substances in the world to ingest.) We each get only one body per lifetime; we're responsible for taking good care of it. When we do, our bodies love us for our care—we feel and look better, ongoing.

> *Listen with love to your body's messages. It is telling you all you need to know.*
> **—Louise L. Hay**

"Miracle Diet"

Taking care of yourself—your whole self: body, mind, and spirit—is part of truly accepting and loving yourself just as you are. But, keep in mind, truly accepting and loving yourself just as you are—that is, unconditionally—doesn't happen in a moment. Paradoxically, we are usually able to unconditionally accept and love others faster than we are able to unconditionally accept and love ourselves. For women, I think this is because we are conditioned to be dissatisfied with our bodies and appearances. You can't unconditionally accept and love the whole unless you also unconditionally accept and love all the parts. There's no way around it: You have to learn to love your body.

Before you make up your mind that just because I did it, doesn't mean you can, please read on to discover *how* I did it. Then you'll see that if I could do it—and I did—you can do it, too.

Let me lay it all on the line: I am physically small in stature; I wear fabulous hot stilettos and tight jeans; I can pull off a sashay that turns heads. Please don't close the book, and don't stop reading! My ego has not taken over, and I am not a conceited you-know-what. Just hear me out on this. It doesn't matter what you look like. All that matters is how you feel about yourself, regardless of what you look like. If you're overweight but comfortable with who you are, good for you (as long as you're not under doctor's orders to lose weight; remember, health and safety are first and foremost). It doesn't matter if everyone else thinks you're gorgeous or hideous; *it matters only what you think*. I cannot emphasize this enough.

That brings me to the truth about the miracle diet. This "diet" is so simple that anyone, anywhere and at any time, can follow it. In fact, there is only one thing you need to do to stay on this diet. Aha! Now I *know* I have your attention. All you have to do is drop comparisons. By that I mean, stop comparing yourself to other people. Yes, you read correctly: *That's it*.

Let me just say that this is deceptively simple. While it's true that this is a one-step program, it's also true that the very idea of dropping comparisons is so alien to most Americans that I might as well suggest that you go live on the moon, instead of here on Earth. We use comparisons every single minute of every single day. It's not wrong, but it also isn't natural. We have been conditioned by the media and society to compare ourselves to others; others who are smarter, wealthier, more attractive, or whatever else, as the case may be. In a consumer-oriented society, this is necessary; if we don't feel that we are lacking, we won't buy whatever it is that will make us more fill-in-the-blank(s). Comparison is a necessity of consumerism. Okay. I said I wasn't a biochemist; I'm not a sociologist, a psychologist, or a behavioral theorist, either. But my experiences and observations have taught me that, if you don't have good health and a positive self-image, then whatever else you do have won't be worth much at all. That being said, I can tell you without equivocation that you have to learn how to be comfortable saying the following statement out loud to yourself: I love my body. A lot of women, and even some men, will find this difficult. Do it anyway. Do it until it's not a chore. Do it until you find yourself thinking it without having to tell it to yourself.

I'll start. *I love my body!* Do you know what I love about my body? I love every last stinkin' inch of it. I am in no way saying my body is perfect or fantastic or even good. (Remember, I have given birth to twins.) Even though I can wear tight jeans and sashay in stilettos, it is all smoke and mirrors. By this I mean that all I did was what I'm encouraging you to do. Try it and see what happens. The simple act of dropping comparisons allowed me to accept and love my body—and my entire self—unconditionally. Doing that is the only way to gain self-confidence.

Like most women in our society, I spent most of my life—up until the moment when I put myself on the miracle diet, that is—hating my appearance: my weight, my eyes, my stomach, my thighs, and even my butt. Some would say that I have no butt; I think it makes my tight jeans look good, so who cares what anyone else thinks? Again, every woman in our society is conditioned from girlhood to believe that someone else has at least one "better" body part than she has.

Imagine how liberating it would feel to just let all of that go . . . to just pretend that it doesn't matter. Guess what—you don't have to imagine, and you don't have to pretend. It doesn't matter. If you let it all go, you'll see that it never mattered in the first place. When I did that, it was an aha moment: I realized that, no matter what, there will always be someone who is thinner or taller or prettier, or who has bigger boobs or a nicer butt or better thighs. In other words, there will always be someone to compare yourself to. We think that achieving whatever the object of our comparison has will bring us happiness or fulfillment. But it never will. The only thing that can ever bring us true happiness and lasting fulfillment is accepting and loving ourselves as we are.

Don't get me wrong: It's not easy, and it doesn't come quickly; our programmed brains need to be reconditioned. Nevertheless, with concerted effort and commitment to your well-being, it can be done. I guarantee that, if you follow the miracle diet, you, too, will feel fabulous. Accept and love your body, just as it is—right now. You'll see how quickly you realize that you accept and love all of you, just as you are. You can't imagine how good you will feel when you look in the mirror—into your own eyes in your reflection—and say out loud, "I love my body."

> *Begin to see what is in front of you, rather than what you learned is there.*
> —**Stephen C. Paul**

Reindeer Games

Great—body and body-image healing can be checked off the Awareness To-Do List. Um, yes, that's true. But that doesn't mean all the work's done. Not even close. It's the body/mind/spirit connection, so that's only one out of three. And it's a process, so, in essence, the work is never really done in the sense of what we usually mean by *done*. Better to think of it as an accomplishment. Moving through life with a healthy body and a healthy body image is part of being a healthy person.

Next step: You have to learn to love your mind. This one can actually be trickier than learning to love your body, because our minds constantly bombard us with thoughts and messages that resist—and often contradict—self-acceptance and self-love. Be brave, though, for it must be done.

Yet again, I will assure you, if I could do it—and I did—you can, too. Most important, once you truly and unconditionally accept and love your body and mind, your spirit/soul will show itself to you—and you'll know for sure that you love yourself, because you'll feel the love inside you . . . the universe within, fully engaged with your higher self.

Once I had my body and body image healed, it was time to address my emotional healing. It is so easy to get stuck in our own minds sometimes. I ought to know. That would happen to me whenever I thought—or, more precisely, overthought—and/or made poor judgment calls because I hadn't used my intuition. Trusting our intuition is the first step toward loving our minds.

At about the same time that I was discovering this, I was going weekly to have a urine analysis (UA) as continual proof of staying clean. I had chosen a small, private firm that seemed very comfortable, but it was a bit of a drive to get there. Court-ordered or not (mine was not), a UA is monitored or observed by the tester in order to ensure that the person being tested is not trying to alter the sample and/or test in any way. Such monitoring/observing usually included a woman standing in front of me, staring at me, and watching my hands while I was on the pot. Talk about invading my personal space! I had tried a few different firms before finally settling on the one I mentioned, which was not at all creepy, dirty, or filled with sleazy guys in the lobby—it was worth driving farther to get there.

Kathryn, the owner of the testing facility, was always on the premises. I liked her instinctively; she was very friendly and never judgmental. A few weeks had passed, and she and I would chat during my weekly visits. Each time I went, we chatted a little longer; our conversations grew deeper, evolving from everyday events, the news, and health/exercise regimens to life and our individual places in it. "The meaning of life," you might say. We talked about what mattered to each of us, and how yoga and the study of synchronicity and other universal mysteries were enriching our lives. I felt we were connecting on a spiritual level.

One day Kathryn said something that struck a chord deep within me: "Brienne," she said, "if you want the answer to a question, just ask the universe."

"What kind of question?" I asked.

"It doesn't matter. Any question."

That sounded simple enough. Perhaps *too* simple. I must have looked doubtful, or at least ambivalent.

"I can tell you're a little dubious," she laughed. "Let me expand a bit on what I just said. You have to have a clear and open mind." I nodded that I could do that; we had already discussed yoga and synchronicity. She continued, "You ask by declaring the truth of your desire."

"Okay."

"I'm serious. You could say, 'Why am I here?' Then, all you have to do is wait for the answer to show up or manifest. Try it. You'll see what I mean."

While driving home, I mulled a question over in my mind and decided, why not? I mean, the worst thing that could happen was I wouldn't get an answer. So, why not just ask the universe for my answer?

Remember how I said that I found spirituality in the same place where I peed in a cup? Well, this was how it happened. I stated my question out loud: "How long until I feel like I'm really doing okay?" (I decided not to start with anything as deep as, "Why am I here?") For good measure, I repeated my question out loud again, just in case the universe wasn't listening. About twenty minutes later, I heard the answer in the lyrics of a song playing on the radio. It was just a pop song about love and trust taking time, and not rushing things. I felt chills shoot up and down my spine, and a very strange sensation surged through my body. In that instant, I knew not only that I was receiving my answer from the universe but also that I wasn't supposed to play games anymore.

This was it, the real deal. *Ask, and you shall receive.* Make sure you're ready.

> *You are a child of the universe . . . you have a right to be here.*
> **—Max Ehrmann, "Desiderata"**

7

Calling the Universe

Hello, Universe? It's Me . . . Again

Maybe you're thinking that you'll feel more than a little silly asking the universe questions—especially if you ask out loud. I hear you; I felt a little awkward at first, too. Certainly, we wouldn't want to talk to the universe while we're out and about throughout the day—even I only asked my questions out loud when I was alone, at home or in my car. Once you try it, though, the process kind of grows on you. In fact, at the beginning of this kind of connection with the universe—and with our higher selves—the feeling we get when we receive the answer is so powerful that we feel compelled to keep asking. Part of this, I guess, is that we're afraid to stop asking, because if we do, the answers might stop coming to us.

For me, added to this was the feeling that I wasn't quite sure it was safe to trust the seemingly bizarre appearances of both gifts and givers. I was making progress learning to trust by using my intuition, but I still had doubts.

The universe, however, had its own plans for me. And my higher self was in complete cahoots. Yes, again—I had to learn the hard way.

We've all heard the advice from multiple sources about how easy it is to reap the gifts of all one's hopes and dreams by simply asking for them. The discouraging part is that, when we hear about this, we focus on the hope or dream as it appears in our minds, and when it doesn't quickly manifest in exactly the way we imagined, we become very frustrated. So frustrated that we abandon the idea of asking and return to our habitual thinking

71

patterns. What we don't realize—because no one has ever clearly explained it to most of us—is that the problem does not lie in the asking, but rather, in the expectation that we will receive exactly what we imagined. Asking the universe entails trusting the universe to manifest what we need—not what we think we need.

This is a big concept to grasp and accept. But, yes, the universe does know better than we do. No matter how dark a place we are in, we are never alone. Yet sometimes we have to go down deep in order to come out of the darkness. This is the same as saying that addicts usually need to hit bottom, and also that the only way out is usually the way through.

Not everyone is willing to abandon security. That simply means facing all our fears and demons—addictions and otherwise—and being willing to open up and stop judging. It also means being willing to see past the superficial layers of judgment and comparison and the other day-to-day thought processes that absorb an inordinate amount of time and energy; to go deeper than all that, to where the true individual—the higher self—resides. It means to live with soul, to love unconditionally.

Simply stated, "Yes, I loved cocaine." I didn't want to give it up because it gave me so much energy and "helped" me fulfill the duties of the crazy whirlpool of living I had created. If I had truly accepted and loved myself, I would never have turned to cocaine, or anything else, to try to get through my life, because I would have realized that my life, as I was living it at that point, was no longer a reasonable or normal one. It is neither reasonable nor acceptable for normal mommies to use cocaine in order to manage myriad extracurricular activities, take care of the kids and the house, look fabulous 24/7—and, don't forget, make those fantastic cupcakes all the time. I mean, exactly what would be so horrifying if makeup went unapplied, a hair was out of place, dinner was five minutes late, or cupcakes weren't frosted to camera-ready perfection? The answer, of course, is nothing. There is absolutely nothing horrifying about any of that. What is horrifying is that anyone would think that any of that was so important that he or she would use drugs—or induce any form of self-harm—in order to accomplish it, or feel like a failure because it could not be accomplished. All that being said, the reality is this: I needed to stand tall, face my addiction, and address the real emotional problems feeding it. *Who wants to face their emotions and cry nonstop for weeks? Who wants to feel abandoned, lonely, sorrowful, and desperate for forgiveness?* Actually, no one I know. I certainly didn't want to—but I knew I *had to.*

The more we see, the more we are capable of seeing.
—**Maria Mitchell**

Presto!—It Really *Is* Magic

Remember, it's all about steps. One step at a time. First you awaken, and then you become aware. You have to look and hear, with your heart and mind open, before you can really see and listen—before you can absorb what you've seen and heard. You have to ask—with your heart and mind open to what is best for you and meant for you—before you can receive. And remember that what *is* best for you and meant for you might not necessarily be what you *think* is best for you and meant for you.

Yes, I know, it's a lot of steps; but shortcuts usually don't take us where we really need to go, or where we're meant to be. Even magic only looks like magic—it's really the result of believing in the powers of the universe, which includes believing in yourself.

Before I describe this part of my journey any further, let me explain that this was not something I was ready to take on quickly. In fact, my first few steps were pretty shaky, but then I dove in. I unleashed on my therapist, Dr. Dani, every bad and crummy thing I had ever done, thought, or said in the course of my life. By saying it all out loud, I released it from my mind and body, and then I was able to begin to lighten up.

With Dr. Dani's guidance and my own introspection, I was gaining an understanding of how my actions directly affected people in the most minute situations. For example, if I am in a bad mood and snap at the gas-station attendant, he will then accumulate my negative thoughts and energy. Now his mood and energy have shifted because of me, without his even realizing it. At the end of the day, he goes home and snaps at his wife or kids. They, in turn, feel hurt or insecure because of his anger, which is not even related to them or to him. I'm sure you get the idea: All our energy absorption and dissemination has a trickle-down effect through our interactions. Most often, we are not even aware of what we are doing.

But wait—it is not bleak by any means. All it takes to positively alter these results is an internal adjustment on our part. By shifting our thought processes and actions to something positive from something negative, we each can make a world of difference. Let's take another example. Say I am working as a customer-service rep for a retail company. A disgruntled customer calls, yelling and degrading me because she hasn't received her order on time, and insisting that I drop everything I am doing in order to attend to her problem. At the same time, I receive a phone call from a very nice and patient customer, who is willing to be put on hold to await the results of my investigation of her order's status. Which customer do you think I will want to assist? Definitely *not* the one who berated me, indicating by her words and tone that she was blaming me personally for her problem. That negative energy (from caller number one) would have unintentionally affected me all day. However, the positive energy (from sweet and kind caller number two) also would have stayed with me throughout the day—but in a different way, because it would have made me feel good, not bad. Positive experiences, however seemingly insignificant, create positive energy; likewise for negative ones. An inner shift from negative to positive can result in a day spent smiling, feeling comfortable and comforted, and just happy and good in general. This kind of shift can have such a result not just on us, but on everyone we interact with, deeply or superficially. Pretty simple thing to do, given the exponential benefits, huh? How's that for each of us healing the world!

So, yes, energy that is healing, loving, and comfortingly warm can elevate moods and clear negative thought processes. My gift of these newfound abilities to understand, develop, and use positive energy felt like magic. I guess *magic* might sound like a stretch or an exaggeration, but that really is how it felt to me—it still does. It's like finding the key to a door with a treasure behind it, and then realizing that we all have equal access and right to the treasure; it's ours to share, as long as we realize that we each have the key, and no one has the right to hoard. Hmmm . . . pretty powerful and amazing stuff. What better word to describe it than *magic?*

> *Try to avoid looking forward or backward, and try to keep looking upward.*
>
> **—Charlotte Brontë**

[**A word about therapy:** *Okay, quite a few words. I think therapists can be extremely helpful, but there are other ways to accomplish this lightening up. I am in no way trying to imply that I have the expertise or credentials to offer mental-health advice or assess the abilities of any provider of mental-health care, nor is this meant to endorse or discourage mental-health care or counseling. All I am trying to do is explain that there are many different options for and approaches to personal growth and self-help, and we each need to find the one that works for us, seeking professional advice as needed. My therapist helped me tremendously; other methods work equally well for other* *people. It's a very individual choice. One thing that can work well for people, regardless of whether they are in therapy or not, is keeping a journal. The act of writing things down can have the same effect as saying them out loud. (A word of caution here: It doesn't matter if you keep a journal on the computer or write your thoughts in a notebook; the point of keeping a journal is that it's a safe and private place to collect your thoughts and feelings. Blogging, which is great for engaging with people, is not the same as keeping a journal, because, when you blog, other people—not just a trusted, trained therapist—are privy to your intimate thoughts, and you might regret that later.) Again, journaling is something you can try—or not. See if it resonates for you; if it does, great—if not, try something else until you discover what "clicks" for you. You'll know when you find what's right for you.]*

Asked and Answered—Now What?

You ask and get answers. You find the key that opens the door. You turn negative to positive. You experience the magic. It's all great. Life is better than you ever dreamed it would be, or at least you recognize that it *could be*—that it *will be,* as soon as you fill-in-the-blank(s).

Are you kidding me? If you get the answers and feel the magic, how is life not automatically better? Simply because life isn't stagnant. It changes. Every day is new, filled with promise and potential, which also means that something bad can, and often does, happen. No matter how much we grow and evolve, we still have to live every day. There is no picture-perfect postcard image of life that shines behind the emblazoned "The End" as the movie fades out to the happily-ever-after we know does not exist.

However, the process of living is an adventure and a gift. We ask, and we are answered. No matter what happens, it will be okay, because we can trust ourselves and the universe to know what to do, even if we don't know how it will all turn out. Faith is positive energy, not a signed guarantee. When you really believe in yourself and in the universe—when you really have faith—you won't need a signed guarantee. You will just live.

I completely understand and respect that you might be thinking, *Um . . . okay.* But, one day, it does just happen the way I described. For me, it was when I finally realized why I was being called to this particularly tough duty. I had so many visions and voices telling me the reasoning behind it. I still feel weird saying that "I was told" the answer. But I was. And as soon as I believed it once I was told, I was able to resolve a lot of inner issues.

I don't expect you to just take my word for it. Let me show you how it happened. First of all, we have to understand that the power behind manifestation—that is, the "answer" that comes when we "ask"—is our acknowledgment of its strength. This is something that you have to feel for yourself without overthinking it. Basically it means that if you don't believe you will receive an answer, you might not—or you will, but you won't believe it. See what I mean? By acknowledging the strength of manifestation—by believing, trusting, and having faith—we accept its power, and then it manifests.

Really? Yes, really. As I further explored this power, there were several times when I thought about something in a deep and focused way—asking the universe to weigh in—and, amazingly, my answer would appear within the next day. One particular day I became a little arrogant about this serious magic power. (I know we're supposed to share it, but at that point in the process, I was still learning, and initial access can make all of us a little giddy.) Anyway, as I was driving that day, I would ask to hear a particular song on the radio. No sooner did I ask than, sure enough, that song would play. The more this happened, the more I kept asking for insignificant things like that to prove to myself that I was engaging with the universe and accessing the power of manifestation. Every time it happened, I told myself inwardly, *Yes! This is really happening.*

Before you start to think that I misused the power of the universe, instead of just buying an MP3 player, that's not at all the point I'm trying to make. The point is that it is not necessarily what you ask for that matters; what matters is the deep truth that lies behind your intentions. In other words, you might be granted your wish for a million dollars, but the greed and extravagance behind asking might also turn your life into a nightmare. You might have been better off never wishing for the million dollars to come into your life, because it ended up causing more pain and damage than you ever would have had without the money. Part of the power of manifestation is that the universe knows better than we do, and it gives us what we need when we need it. If we press too hard, we may get a lot more than we bargained for, hence the adage, "Be careful what you wish you for; you might get it." By all means, ask; but, by all means, also accept that when something doesn't manifest, you should be grateful for that, too. Don't be disappointed by this. It just means that we have to trust in that which is stronger and wiser than we are. Stay open, and see what happens.

Many people believe that they do not have any psychic powers or intuition. I have heard this countless times, and, no doubt, you have, too. In reality, every single person and living thing has access to these powers, because these are the powers of the universe, of which we all are a part. Even my old toothless, flatulent pug dog has an intuitive sense—as do all pets and animals, if you look closely enough to see it. I observe my dog using her intuitive sense all the time: when she stays extremely close and cuddles up to me because I am not feeling well; when she barks in the night because she hears or feels something (although her bark is more of a geriatric huffing and puffing than a warning cry). And when my infant twins came home for the first time, she was never jealous; if I left the room, she would move in and sit close to them, as if acting like a replacement mother until I came back in, when she moved away to give me my space back. She uses her intuition to know when to guard, when to protect, and when to love—not to mention when a food crumb hits the floor thirty feet away from her. Just like animals, people possess a deep sense of intuitiveness; it isn't that we don't have it, it's just that we don't all discover it at the same point in life—or that over time we forget we possess it, because children can be observed using intuition quite frequently.

As with anything else, reclaiming our intuition happens differently for each of us. Prior to my embarking on this part of my journey—or the universe's placing me there, depending upon how you look at it—I had often heard that during times of intense stress or trauma, some people are awakened, and then they step into their powers and truth as human beings. In other words, extreme circumstances can trigger us to become our higher selves. Let me repeat that I have no professional training to back up these statements—I am not a provider of medical or mental-health care—nor am I advocating any type of religious belief or practice. I am merely sharing my experiences, what did and didn't work for me, and how I handled the process.

At one point I hit an emotional low. I am talking *really* low. I not only remember how low I felt, I can actually still feel it. I felt like such a failure that I did not want to tell anyone how far down I had fallen—even my therapist. I felt like I was out on a limb, dangling all by myself, with no one to confide in. I could actually *feel* my heart hurt; that's the pain I described still being able to feel, even now. Anyway, at that point I said out loud, "Please help me. I just don't know what to do."

I was so low that I started to question my newfound connection to the universe, thinking I was just being arrogant when I believed that the songs I heard on the radio appeared because I'd requested them. I started to feel skeptical about receiving an answer. I doubted that I could trust the answer I received, if I even did receive one, because these were not real answers—just my own arrogance. But then I thought about James and Kathryn, and all I'd been learning and feeling. I decided to give it one more shot. I asked more questions—not song requests, just simple questions. Each and every time, I received the answer to the question I'd asked in the form of a song playing on the radio. I began to realize that the universe was using the radio to communicate with me, just as it used other methods with other people. The radio, I guess, just worked for me.

In any case, my stress level was at its peak one afternoon when I was scheduled to meet my attorney to discuss the epic legal battle in which I was entangled with my soon-to-be ex-husband over our impending divorce. In the weeks prior to this meeting, I had been experiencing anxiety—complete with daily vomiting, my hair falling out, and many nights of waking up in a cold sweat because of horrific nightmares (no more black tongue, but the rest of it was more than I could deal with). In a nutshell, I was at the breaking point, physically and emotionally—I could not, and did not want to, continue.

However, if I just stopped now, it would mean an unsure financial future, not just for me but also for my kids. Sacrificing my own security was one thing; sacrificing theirs was quite another. Nevertheless, I had reached the point where my health and happiness were not worth jeopardizing for a few bucks—and neither were theirs, and a mother-in-meltdown cannot benefit her children. Let me clarify that it was never about the money; it was the principle of fairness that I was fighting for. So, that same afternoon, before I got in the car, I begged for a sign to reassure me that my decision to drop the case was the right thing to do.

I drove a few blocks down the road before I turned on the car radio. The next song that played had a sweet and slow melody, and the lyrics proclaimed that the only way to handle your troubles is to let things go and turn out the way they are meant to. I knew right then and there that all I had to do was open up and allow trust and faith to guide me. I felt like a two-ton brick had been lifted off my shoulders. I could breathe and stand tall again. I was so relieved. I felt calm and elated at the same time. Even more than that, I just knew intuitively that the path I was on, no matter how bizarre it might seem, was the right one for me.

No one can give you better advice than you give yourself.
—**M. Tullius Cicero**

Law of Attraction

The law of attraction, in the simplest terms, states that "like attracts like"—for good or ill. It's all part of the negative-to-positive energy shifting I described earlier. At this point in the process, I felt more positive than negative, but there still was a significant amount of negativity in my life. Granted, a certain portion of it was outside my control, so the best I could do was practice the shift-to-positive mode. I was about to recognize that I needed to purge the energy that was beyond my ability to shift from negative to positive.

It happened like this. At that point in my life, I had a persistent feeling that's hard to put into words. The best way I can describe it is this: *I know I'm close to figuring things out, but I just can't put my finger on it—particularly in regard to a job or career.* The job/career issue was one of growing concern. I had been out of school for quite a while and a stay-at-home mom for some time after that, so my résumé looked like it needed more than just an overhaul. I was so lost as to what path to take that I felt like I was spinning around in circles. I practiced calm so I wouldn't start feeling overwhelmed, but I honestly had no idea what to do about finding the right job or figuring out which career path to choose.

In the midst of all this, I went to lunch with my brother.

As the waitress set down our plates, I had just finished telling him that I didn't know what to do. "Do I go back to school?" I asked him.

"You could do that," he said, munching on a French fry.

"I could, I guess," I agreed dubiously, raking my salad with my fork but not taking a bite. "But I need a job that's flexible so I can spend time with the kids."

He nodded, knowing it was essential for me to have as much time as possible with my children.

I crunched a piece of romaine and looked at my brother. He didn't say anything, but he knew me like a book, so I figured he already knew what I was thinking: *No employer is going to jump at the chance to hire someone with my lack of recent experience, plus all my requirements.* I had not shared with my brother my recently embraced belief system, knowing that his naturally practical nature might make him skeptical. That didn't impact my own faith in my belief system one bit, though; I held tight to that: *Whatever it is that I am intended to do, it will be coming soon.* I knew that, and I trusted that, with all my heart and soul. But I still needed a job.

I sipped water from my glass as I waited for my ever-logical older brother to answer.

After what felt like hours but was really only a moment or two, he said, "Brienne, go see a life coach who can help you figure out what you want to do. Career-wise, I mean."

Imagine my surprise hearing the words *life coach* come out of my brother's mouth! I thought he might offer me a shot of wheatgrass next. (He didn't. But a while later, when I broached the subject of the power of manifestation, synchronicity, and other truths of the universe, I was met with an equally pleasant surprise: My perennially practical older brother was also infinitely cool and open-minded. Who knew? Even older brothers can become aware!) Okay, back to that conversation. It took me by surprise that not only was he open to the idea of a life coach, but he was actually suggesting that I go to see one.

"Can I tell you stories about *that!*" he said, going on to recount numerous ones about his and his wife's friend, Alisa. A life coach, indeed, Alisa had helped many people recharge their lives. "I'm not kidding. Literally every single person I know who has gone to Alisa said she's amazing. Working with her changes people's lives—for the better and forever."

"Okay, okay! I'm in," I told him. I didn't need anything more than my brother's assurance of Alisa's "phenomenal success rate." If he said that she could improve and transform my life into the one I'd always dreamed of, that was enough for me.

The only remaining question was this: "Where do I sign up?"

My brother gave me Alisa's card, which listed her website and phone number. We hugged goodbye, and we each went about the rest of our day. When I got home, I immediately went to the computer to check out Alisa's site. All the reviews were testaments to her unique abilities. Each and every one stated that she had helped the person positively transform his or her life. I fell asleep that night feeling a deep sense of peace. Synchronicity was alive and well and hard at work in my life. With Alisa's help, I knew I would find my right career path.

The following day, I called and made an appointment to see Alisa at Awake in Joy, her consulting, coaching, and meditation studio. What was to follow in the next few weeks was exactly what my brother had predicted—it would change my life forever. "For the better" is a monumental understatement. It was at Alisa's studio that my dreams began to assemble themselves into a form that would soon become a reality. *My reality.*

Over the next few weeks and under Alisa's guidance, I filled out questionnaires and wrote essays to narrow down the general field in which I wanted to focus. She never once told me what to do; she raised questions and then encouraged me to explore. The more I thought about what I wanted to do, the more things just seemed to fall into place. I kept going around in circles and feeling vague about a career.

That's when Alisa asked, "If you could have your absolute dream job— no rules, just your perfect dream job—what would that be, Brienne?"

Without hesitating or even needing to think about it, I replied, "I want to be a writer and an artist, but c'mon, who really does that for a living?"

Alisa smiled. "*You* can, if that's what you really want."

Working with a life coach might not be the right choice for you, for any number of reasons. There are a lot of ways to get your life back on track. Meditating, yoga, and life coaching worked best for me; keeping a journal, mind mapping, and focused visualization might work better for someone else. Still others might opt to buy a career-planning book or research career paths online. It's not about any one way; it's about the way that resonates for each of us. I left the studio beaming, even though I lacked the concrete details of how I would make this happen. I just knew that I could, and would, do it. Alisa didn't help me just by offering guidance. She also helped me by believing in me—just as Tina had.

At this point, I made up my mind that I was wholeheartedly going to dive into a new way of discovering myself—who I was because of what I'd done up that point, as well as because of what I was meant to do now . . . *what I was going to do now.* That brought me to the next major move that I made.

When leaving in-patient rehab as a recovering addict, one is supposed to participate in an intensive out-patient care program, which consists of attending meetings, both with a counselor and in a support group. I stayed in my program for a while but soon decided that this was a program I needed to leave. Again, I am in no way knocking these programs, which are successful for many people. I'm simply stating that it just didn't work for me, and here's why: I felt like I was being suffocated by dark forces. The men at the meetings preyed on young women, there were drug deals in the parking lot, and it seemed that the attendees refused to speak or think in an optimistic way. When I attended these meetings, I felt vulnerable, scared, and depressed; so, before too long, I figured that this wasn't helping me.

Working with Alisa reaffirmed this for me. What I needed to do was surround myself with people who were positive, optimistic, and healthy; people who could, and would, support, promote, and guide my healing process. And so I did exactly what I needed to do.

> *The best way to secure future happiness is to be as happy as is rightfully possible today.*
>
> **—Charles W. Eliot**

Lost—and Found—in Space

My journey now began moving into the realm of deeper connection with the universe. Through my work with Alisa, I was learning how to move beyond self-sabotage; find my center and ground myself; and feel and practice gratitude. I discovered that all these concepts and practices were necessary for effective recovery, as well as for true and meaningful personal growth and conscious living as my higher self. It was a lot of inner work, and the concepts were very deep, but I loved every bit of it.

In retrospect, I might have been going too deep too quickly, but everything happens for a reason—not just what we do, but the way we do it. I had to follow my path in my own way.

My days were now spent thinking about guidance—about the universe and God—and about what I was supposed to be doing. My "life's true calling," some might say. This was a shift, because I had been thinking of the universe as separate from God up to this point; God, in my thoughts, was part of the Catholic upbringing that I considered as going against my newfound wisdom and the philosophies I was currently embracing. At that point, I didn't feel that I would be unconditionally accepted, protected, and loved by God; the universe I was engaging with was a loving force that was separate from the religion I had been raised in and continued to believe in pre-rehab. What I still needed to learn was that spirit and religion, paradoxically, do not always mesh.

As I've said, I hadn't quite learned all I needed to yet, but I was making progress. Good progress, day by day. Throughout the week that followed, I spent my evenings writing in my journal (yes, I journal, too!) and thinking about the word *God*. Just the word. That brought me to the conclusion that my pre-rehab Catholic roots had served me well, but now it was time for me to get to a deeper spiritual level. In order to do that, I had to break away from the fear that I was going to hell for my sins. Whether because of the soul-engaging explorations I'd done up to that point or because it was just my moment to take hold of my own power, I will never know; all I do know is that, somehow, I *knew* I wasn't going to hell for my sins. (Granted, I won't know that for sure until the day I actually do pass on, but it is how I felt at that point, and it's how I feel now.)

I then realized that what I needed to do, what was the best I could do, was just talk to God. That's right, just talk effectively and honestly—talk to him/them/whomever God was—in my own words. The more I thought about it, the more comfortable I felt that this was right for me. Next I realized that I felt more comfortable thinking of God as spirit—rather like the Native Americans who refer to God as "The Great Spirit." That's when I started to feel a real connection between knowing that I still needed to get clarity on a lot of things—including what to do for a living—but still feeling innately sure that I was on the right path.

Okay, so I felt sure I was on the right path, but I still had to get on track. We can think and explore and engage, and all that deep stuff is fantastic—and I love every minute of it—but, at the end of the day, the only way that what needs to get done can get done is to do it. And the only one who can do it is each of us—you, me, and everyone else—in our own lives. I knew that, but I still needed to put it into practice. Because the wisdom and guidance I was accepting and trying to figure out how to use were all so utterly new to me, I just didn't know how to put the two of them together, practically speaking. I knew how to think about my connection to the universe, but I didn't know how to use it to find a way to make a living. The moment comes for all of us when we have to not just know what we know but also *live* what we know.

Added to that was the fact that I had been so immersed in the divorce and so focused on how terrible it was that I had closed off my heart, without even realizing that I had done so. I was communicating with the universe and trusting the answers I received, but I had lost my connection to gratitude and trust. I know this sounds strange, given that I continued to have an innate sense that I was going to be fine—and also given that I continued to trust my feelings and follow them wherever they led me, even though I was logically questioning everything. It felt strange to me, too, but I did just trust it. I knew that a key to the mystery was still missing; I just didn't know what it was. I know now, of course, that it was God—my connection to love and trust and gratitude was just incomplete without loving and trusting and thanking God—God *and* the universe, not either one without the other. That was the key to living what I knew.

It was then that I began to take energy work seriously. I couldn't wait to regroup with Alisa.

The next time I saw her, I told her all about my adventures writing about God (as in, the word) and spirit.

Alisa smiled that smile, so I knew wisdom was to follow.

"You're ready to meditate, Brienne," she told me.

"I do meditate. Remember the meditative yoga I do?"

"This is different. It's much more spiritually focused."

"Okay," I nodded, not sure where she was going, but trusting it would work for me, because I trusted Alisa. Everything she suggested resonated, and I knew she and her guidance were right for me.

"Good. We'll start with a simple meditation that will open up your mind. Once we accomplish that, we'll be able to build the depth of your meditations from that point."

I nodded.

"Are you ready to try it now?"

I nodded again.

"Good. You should keep the first one to about twenty minutes. Start when you feel ready. I'll leave you alone, but you can stop when you feel it's been about twenty minutes. Come get me when you're done, and we can talk about how it felt." I nodded okay, and she continued. "Whenever you feel ready, just close your eyes. Think about gratitude. When you lose focus, simply bring your mind back to center. Keep thinking about gratitude."

That sounded simple enough, and I already had some experience from the meditative yoga I'd been doing. I accepted Alisa's having said it wasn't the same, but I figured I had to have at least a sliver of experience more than someone who'd never done anything meditative. So, I closed my eyes and relaxed, waiting for inspiration to flood my mind, lead me down an illuminated path—mentally speaking, that is.

Well, not exactly. Actual meditation was nothing like meditative yoga. Nothing at all. My first attempt at meditation went something like this: After I closed my eyes and took a couple of cleansing breaths, waiting for the inspirational flood of illumination, I thought about my grocery list. After that, I thought about the last magazine article I had read, and then about my kids and what we had planned to do over the weekend. At that, my mind started to race in a zillion different directions. *Will we have enough time to go to the park this weekend? Or to visit my brother and his family? Hmmm. I don't know . . . maybe I'll pack our swimsuits, just in case . . . the kids will be upset if they can't go in the hot tub. Will we really do all that? No, we'll probably just have lunch and take an afternoon nap. Mmm, a nap . . . that sure sounds good. I would love to take a nap right now . . . I am so-o-o-o relaxed. . . . Wait! Did I change the sheets this morning when I remembered I needed to? I think I did, but I'm not sure. I left something in the dryer, but I can't remember what it was. Did I leave the dryer running? I hope not—no, I'm sure I shut it off before I left the house. I always do. Yes, I did, I definitely shut it off, because a lint puff got on my black pants . . . I remember picking it off. No clue what's in the dryer, but it is definitely not running. What about the sheets? And the grocery list . . . did I remember everything? . . .*

That took about three breaths; we don't realize how rapidly our thoughts cycle. I struggled to remember what Alisa had said, but it was harder to do than I thought it would be, given that she'd only provided me with the instructions a few moments before.

Okay. Stop. Bring it back to center . . . center, yeah—center of what—center of my brain or center of myself? What is the center of my brain? Is that the thinking part or the personality part? Is it the soul part, or is that my heart? Is it the center of my heart, then, not my brain at all? I am so confused. I should have asked Alisa more questions and not felt so cocky about my meditative yoga experience. Center . . . center . . . there was something about gratitude, too. What was that again? Uh-oh. Wait. Stop. Did I pick up my package downstairs? This is important . . . I need that package. I also need to meditate, but I can't think . . . I can't focus. How do I center? How am I supposed to know what to do?

It went on and on like that for what felt like forever. I finally decided that this meditation session, which I was certain was almost over, had not been very productive. *Maybe it was because I let it go so much longer than twenty minutes. I'll mention that to Alisa.* With that, I opened my eyes and looked at the clock. Three minutes had passed. *Three minutes?* It felt like I had been sitting there for days—at least an hour. How could it possibly have been only three minutes? How could I possibly sit here and do this for twenty minutes? This was just not going to work. This did not feel like an awakening experience; it felt like what I imagined deliberately slow and painful torture would feel like. I had never understood how Chinese water torture worked until my first attempt at meditation.

No need to panic or overreact, I told myself. *Just go back to Alisa and talk to her about what happened. She'll understand, and she'll know what to do.*

I walked through the studio until I found Alisa. "I know it's nowhere near twenty minutes, but I just . . . um . . . couldn't center."

"Don't worry about that, Brienne. It takes practice. Just keep at it. You'll see."

"But, Alisa, I couldn't *find* the center. I'm not sure where it even is."

"Finding where it is for you is part of the meditative process. You'll find it. It takes time."

She seemed awfully calm about my complete cluelessness, so I figured it was okay.

"Practice some more at home between now and the next time we meet. You'll see; you'll get it. Trust me."

I did. Of course I did. We said goodbye, and I headed home.

I practiced. Several times. None of these practices were an improvement on my first attempt. I was convinced that I was the first and probably only student of meditation who actually developed panic attacks trying to practice calm and centering. Why didn't this happen during meditative yoga? When I practiced that, I was completely calm and, well, *centered.* Hmmm.

Next time I met with Alisa, I related all this to her.

She laughed. "You're not having a panic attack; you're just trying too hard."

Trying too hard? How could I try too hard to center and be calm? Even if I were, wouldn't it make me calmer and more centered—the trying too hard, I mean? I didn't say any of this out loud.

"Trust yourself, Brienne," Alisa said. "Find the center, and then focus on it. Your mind wanders, and you bring it back. It's a process."

"Okay, Alisa. But as soon as I start to go into the mediation, just as I get deep in thought, I remember that my closet needs new shelves. Or that I dusted, but I didn't really pick up every picture frame to clean underneath, so now I feel guilty. And my refrigerator needs to be cleaned, defrosted, and stocked with healthier foods, because I've been eating too much junk lately. Or—"

"Brienne, stop," Alisa interrupted gently.

"Too much about cleaning. I know I'm a clean freak."

Alisa laughed softly again. "It doesn't matter about the cleaning or anything else. Your thoughts are your thoughts. Meditation is about acknowledging your thoughts—whatever they might be—and then letting them go. When you center, you let go."

Okay. I get it now. Not! I really wanted to "get" meditation because I knew it was part of my path, but I also knew I wasn't getting it.

"Do you follow?" Alisa asked. She was as patient as always.

Realizing that meditation did not come with an instruction manual, I shook my head. "I want to get it, Alisa, I really do. But I just don't. Maybe if you could give me an example of how to stay on track. How to center, I mean."

She explained, "Think of gratitude. That's your centering point. When your mind wanders off, just bring it back to gratitude."

I did vaguely remember her having said something about gratitude before my first meditation, but I didn't see how that was going to help me center. My actual thought in response was, *What the hell does that mean? I have no idea what you're even talking about, Alisa.*

Rather than describe what she said and what I thought in response, I will just share with you how Alisa further broke down the steps of meditating. Good news! Eventually I got it, and I still use this method when I start any meditation. If this resonates for you, go for it; if not, by all means, try something else.

Step One: *Think of gratitude.* This means, think about something you are truly grateful for. When I close my eyes and think of gratitude, I immediately see my two kids' smiling faces. That instantly brings me into a *feeling* of gratitude. Everyone has a think-of-gratitude image; close your eyes and see what comes up in your mind's eye.

Step Two: *Bring your mind back to center.* When your mind starts to wander—and it will, whether to grocery lists or any type of mental reminders—you bring it back to center by focusing on your think-of-gratitude image. So, I stop focusing on my grocery lists and dryer status by bringing back the image of my children's smiling faces to my mind's eye. As soon as I see those smiling faces, I am brought back to center and to my thoughts of gratitude. Find the think-of-gratitude image that brings you back to center.

That's it—two steps. Meditation is really just cycling between these two steps. If you decide to try meditating, see if this works for you.

Once I got the hang of bringing it back to center—and it did take practice—I realized why it had taken me so long to get there. I didn't want to release my fears and open up to unknown thoughts, ideas, or judgments. I was afraid that my mind would show me things I didn't want to see . . . that I was afraid to see. When I finally began to feel safe in my own head, I was able to really dive deep into meditation.

For me, the purpose of meditation was to close off the world and quietly listen to what my heart and mind were telling me . . . and watch, without judgment, what they were showing me. To put it another way, the purpose of meditation was to let go and trust. That kind of unconditional trust, despite all my inner work, was still something I had to practice, but I was more than willing to learn.

And, wow, did I learn. There were many times that I literally had to excuse myself so that I could give myself five minutes of peace and quiet, and then I would find center and ask what I should do to resolve whatever problem was bothering me. This helped me consider things before I made decisions or acted on my thoughts. Sometimes my mental considering involved an inward struggle or sense of triumph—false or otherwise; other times it led to an almost instantaneous feeling of, "Yes, this is right for me." It might seem weird, but taking a time-out has worked for me. I look forward to these time-outs as much as my kids always hated theirs. More than once, I have pulled into a spot in a store parking lot, put the car in park, and then asked out loud, "Hey . . . I need some help on this one. What do I do?"

I always get an answer. Usually it's in the form of an image of something that relates to the situation I'm working on. There have been times that I received a picture that's not something my ego wanted to see. Upon seeing the unwanted image, I would think something like, *Really? Seriously, I mean, c'mon. Fine. Okay, fine.*

This mental sarcasm usually had to do with facing some emotional battle that I had been turning a blind eye to, hoping that ignoring it would make it go away. Nothing doing. I don't get rosy pictures or perfect solutions every time I ask for help—far from it—and I have received plenty of answers that I didn't necessarily want to hear. But I always received an answer, and it was always the answer I needed. And it was always right. As in, dead-on right. Deep down, I always knew that it was right, and that I needed to hear or see it, no matter how much it hurt or how much I hated it. I came to see that the more it hurt and the more I hated it, the more I needed to hear or see whatever it was.

By the point that I started pulling into parking spaces and asking questions out loud in the manner I just described, I had come a long way in my meditation practice. I was now beginning to get in touch with my guides. The more I read and researched other people who had been through emotionally traumatic experiences that were similar to mine, the more I began to feel at ease with the answers. It sank in that, no matter what and without question, there would always be someone there for me—all I had to do was ask for help. My guide—my guardian angel (whom I still had yet to meet) —was always there, willing to help, wanting to help, and eager to help.

It was during a guided (no pun intended) meditation geared toward my calling upon my guides that I actually figured all this out. Up to that point, as I said, I had never met my guides. I just felt a general sense that someone was always there. I thought that a person had only one guide, a sort of guardian angel. It turns out that every single soul on this planet has several guides (a kind of "council"), an entire hierarchy of angels, and a direct line to the Great Spirit. *A council?* you may be wondering. I wondered, too. I could picture them sitting around, shooting the breeze about how clueless I was. They were probably laughing about how I was always stumbling around and second-guessing myself until they gave me an obvious sign that was impossible to miss—even for me.

During the first guide-searching meditation, I was pleasantly surprised by how quickly one of my guides came to me. Not only could I see her, I also could hear her every word. My surprise quickly gave way to excitement, because she was ecstatic that I had finally found her. It was as if she were saying, "Finally! Let's get to work."

She didn't speak to me, per se. I received thoughts and images, and from them I collected the information that she communicated to me on the spiritual level. Her name was Virginia, and she would always be there whenever I called her.

"How will I know when you're there? Can you give me some sort of sign when I call for you?"

I felt her giggle and say, "Oh, you'll know, Brienne. You'll know."

She appeared to be about twenty-five years old and looked like she'd stepped out of a 1920s flapper portrait, complete with bobbed hair that was dark and wavy, over which she wore a crinkled scarf that she tied around her head in a way that was as stylish now as it had been then. I immediately felt at ease in her presence; she simultaneously energized and inspired me when I felt her giggle again and then throw her head back with big laughs that felt warm and welcoming. I loved her style and her sense of humor, but, most of all, I loved the way she made me feel happy and comforted just by being in her presence. Most important, she talked to me in a way that I could understand and grasp; she loved dropping the f-bomb (remember, the real f-word is *fear*) just as much as I did. It wasn't like a too-out-there-I-can't-get-this spiritual experience. What it was, was coming home—to me . . . to my higher self.

I had other guides, but I wouldn't meet them until months later, when I hit an all-time emotional low (more about that in a bit).

> *One day you must leap or fall into the arms of the universe.*
> **—Stephen C. Paul**

Bottom's Up!

Of all the things I've shared and described, this is the hardest. In spite of all the wisdom I'd gained, progress I'd made, and growth I'd achieved, I had to come face-to-face with the fact that I had not made it. Not even close. I had not even hit bottom. Not yet, anyway. But I was about to. I relapsed. And I also had to accept that I *needed* to relapse; I needed to scrape the bottom of the barrel in order to rise up. In order to come home—*really* come home, to God and to my higher self. This is the all-time emotional low I mentioned at the end of the last section.

I used again—both cocaine and alcohol—and that's how I relapsed. It's also how and when the rest of my guides appeared. I had never felt so low in my life. Not only was I confused and ashamed, I also felt as if it were actually *worse* that I relapsed after all I'd learned and how much I'd grown as a person. When I used before, I wasn't awake and aware; this time I was, so what was my problem? I missed completely that I was accomplishing nothing by judging myself. What I still needed to accept was that every choice—good or bad—is part of our journey, no more and no less. This was no different from my deciding that my in-patient rehab mates were more justified in using than I was; that it was "understandable" that they had become addicts, but not that I had. Being an addict was a fact of my life, but it was not my whole life; it was a part of who I was, but it was not all that I was. I was more, much more—I still am, and always will be. I must have felt this at some level, without even knowing I did—wisdom works at subconscious levels once we open to it. I knew I needed to ask for help; I knew that was all I could do at this point. And so, that is what I did.

When you hit bottom—*really* hit bottom, as in, scrape the bottom of the barrel with your face—the only place to go is up.

Sylvia Browne, a well-known author and established expert in the psychic field, explained in one of her books that a person will often go way down in order to come back up. When this is the case, the fall is much deeper and more catastrophic, emotionally and psychologically; as a result, the lessons are much stronger and much more significant. In addition, the person who dives deep in order to rise up seems to be able to rebound even faster and emerge more enlightened. It's as if the universe places profound choices and obstacles directly in front of you. To put it another way, "No guts, no glory." I said at the beginning that life is a journey, and it is—regardless of what we seek. Seeking the higher self is not a pursuit for the faint of heart—especially not when seeking by means of addiction and recovery.

That cataclysmic weekend began with an innocent happy hour at a local tavern. I had met my brother and a few of his coworkers one Friday afternoon to celebrate the start of a great weekend. Having not eaten lunch, I figured I would just snack when I got there and then head out to dinner. Later I was to experience what two beers on an empty stomach can do to a small person—I got wasted. To briefly recap the rest of the evening's events, I essentially became the conductor of a personal train wreck. One bad choice led to another, and before long, I was spiraling out of control. I got drunk; I texted everyone on my phone while drunk; I pissed off a very good friend. But wait, there's more. Here's the grand finale: I went to meet my former drug dealer at a strip club. Even in the thick of it, I kept saying to myself, *Who meets his or her drug dealer at a strip club? Who does this? This is not me. This is not my life. This is not happening.*

The next morning, I woke up with the worst hangover, and I realized that I had to repair the carnage and wreckage of what was left of my personhood, my life, and my integrity. If there were a train-wreck program that passed out merit badges, I would get top honors for self-sabotage. As my thoughts ricocheted around in my hungover brain, I realized that I had completely ruined a relationship with my first truly supportive friend. I was overwhelmed with feelings of self-sabotage, and I hated myself for what I had done.

I kept thinking, *What was last night about? How could I let that happen after all I've done? After all my hard work and all the progress I've made? Why didn't I just ask my guides for help?*

Before I delve into details about the answers to the foregoing *whys*, and what I did about my relapse, let me say one thing: That night was about being an addict. No matter how well you do in recovery, whatever you're addicted to has to stay out of your life forever. As in, *no more, ever.*

A recovering addict cannot have a drink, a snort, a puff. Not even one. Not ever. Period.

I didn't come to that conclusion immediately following my desperate thoughts, but I am sharing it with you because, if you come away from reading this book with one shred of wisdom, that's the one I hope it will be: If you are an addict who stops using, don't ever go back, not even once. As James said to me, "Don't do it. Don't make me see you out there."

My cataclysmic weekend was a turning point for me. It was my dive to the bottom so that I could rise up, stronger and wiser, ready to be the person I was meant to become. As I said, it didn't happen easily or instantly. I didn't go from hungover-in-meltdown to illuminated serenity. With my head splitting, all I could do at first when I woke up the morning after was cry. I cried because I felt so physically ill, but also because I had lost a good friend and shattered my own integrity. What hurt the most, of course, was that it was all the result of nothing but my own conscious choices. I could feel my heart actually hurt, in sharp pains and deep aches. The crying helped a little, but the pain was not letting go of me. I somehow realized that the only way out of this was the way through it. If I didn't face the pain and deal with it, it would destroy me. That's when I knew there was nothing I could do but go straight into a meditation. So, I did what I had to do.

As I've already described my mid-meditation experiences, I am not going to detail these. What we feel during meditation—for those of us who choose to meditate—is a uniquely individual experience, and one that is difficult to capture in words. If you decide to meditate, I hope it brings you as much clarity, joy, and peace as it always brings me. I wish you likewise with whatever else you might choose, so long as it is something that supports and benefits you.

What I do want to share is what I took away from those long hours of meditation, because that profoundly changed my life. Almost immediately, I was more open and more aware, and I saw the cause of my lifelong habit of self-sabotage (something that plagues most, if not all, addicts). I called upon all my guides to help me understand, asking out loud, "What the hell did I just do, and why? Show me why I've been doing what I have with my life. And what I need to do now." As I said, these meditations proved to be very enlightening. In a nutshell, this is the wisdom I received from my guides:

"Brienne, you need to stop drinking and using. You need to stop completely. You need to make total sobriety a part of your life. It's time to stand up for yourself.

"You have sabotaged relationships your whole life because you have no confidence in yourself; you believe you are not worth the relationship. You jumped ship without even trying.

"Stop treating yourself like a commodity. Stop allowing yourself to be used. Be aware of what you deny. Stop judging yourself, because you are the only judge—no one else cares.

"This is your last freebie. Next time, the police will become involved, and you will suffer the consequences."

After receiving all those enlightened messages, I felt like I really understood. Now I could move forward with my healing process and truly succeed; my attempt at healing had been only half-hearted up to now. I needed to be true to myself and true to what I believed in. I needed to stop trying to help others when what they needed to do was help themselves. It wasn't my job to help them; it was my job to help me. "Fixing" others in an attempt to feel accepted never works. All that does work is total, unconditional self-acceptance—*unconditional* means without condition, as in wholly, completely, and truthfully. If that entailed fixing any part of me, that was my prerogative, as long as I accepted and loved myself with or without said fixing.

That was it. I finally felt a sense of peace. I moved from these meditations into my personal power as never before. I felt strong and ready for the challenging road ahead of me.

Amazingly, the friend I thought I'd lost forever called me on Sunday night. "Hey," he said, "are you okay?" I assured him I was, apologizing for the drunk text.

"Don't worry about that. As long as you're okay, that's all that matters." His friendship came through to me in warm, loving waves. I had been so sure that he was out of my life forever; instead, he offered unqualified forgiveness and positive thoughts. "Keep meditating," he encouraged, after I shared some of what I'd experienced. "And don't forget to smile," he added.

"Okay," I said, hesitating a bit. I would try to stay positive, and I did feel a lot better; even so, that last part seemed on the trite side, given what I'd just told him.

He laughed. "SMILE also means Spiritual-Mindedness Is Life Eternal," he explained.

I laughed, too. "I will definitely smile and SMILE," I promised.

We said goodbye, and I hung up.

Throughout my journey, I had stumbled many times. This last time, I had fallen flat on my face. But I had pulled myself to my feet, from the bottom up, and I was going to be okay. Better than okay. I was standing tall and ready for the next step. There was no place to go now but up. And I was ready to soar.

Nothing can bring you peace but yourself.
—**Ralph Waldo Emerson**

Getting Real

Almost immediately, I discovered that the next step was living my truth. This is a lot simpler than it sounds. Part of living in awareness means that you don't practice consciousness just when you're meditating and/or communicating with like-minded individuals. It means that you practice it all the time—even when you're involved with people who are not living sober and/or who are not as conscious as you feel you are, or as you aspire to be. Each of us is at a different point on the journey—and we don't all choose the same path, in the first place. We don't have to persuade others to agree with us, to accept us, or to admire us—remember, it's not our job to fix anyone else, but it's also not our job to make sure anyone acknowledges that we don't need their fixing.

Living our truth simply means being honest with ourselves at every minute of every day. Owning how we feel, what we do, and what we say—including what we think we mess up . . . especially that. No matter how aware we are and how amazing our spiritual awakenings might be—if we choose to pursue that path, and if we have those kinds of experiences—there are still some days when the best we can do is just get through the day. Some days we may feel that we barely do even that; other days are fantastic. Problems, setbacks, and difficult people will always come into our lives, but we don't have to take them into our hearts.

Part of my process was to declare to my family and friends that I was completely sober and clean. I was particularly proud of myself one night when I met my mom for dinner. The cocktail waitress asked for our drink order, and I declined a drink. I felt the full force of my personal power surge through me. After the waitress walked away, I said firmly, "Mom, I am no longer drinking. I am going to remain sober forever, and there is nothing further to discuss about it." Up until my post-cataclysm awareness and strength, I could not have said that; even if I had meant it, the words would have felt empty, and my own voice would have sounded foreign to me.

My mom pleasantly surprised me. "Okay, honey," she said, and then asked, "Wanna split the hummus plate?"

My family does not deal well with heavy-duty issues. Maybe no families do. Maybe dealing well with heavy-duty issues just means getting through whatever it is without falling apart. The point was, I *had* fallen apart and put myself back together. Part of keeping it together entailed accepting that my whole family was partially in denial of what I had been doing. I don't blame my parents. Indirectly, whether they should or not, they felt it all was a reflection of how they had raised me. They had always given me unconditional love and support, but they could not understand that my life was a result of *my* choices. The way they had raised me—and their love and support throughout my life, right up through my mother's response moments before—was part of me, and I was grateful for it, but it didn't control my choices. Only I could do that, for good or ill. I felt really good about what I had just told my mother, and about her response; but I felt even better that I had made some good choices—finally.

Later I was able to do a meditation class with Alisa that proved to be extremely powerful. I received so many messages and was able to hear even more clearly. Also, I reread some tarot card readings from much earlier on in my healing process when I'd asked about my addiction. One of the last things I'd asked during that reading was for insight into why I had been addicted to something that I knew was bad for me. Why was I not able to completely let go of having been addicted, and what was the outcome going to be? The tarot card had declared that the outcome would be a new adventure. I had not understood all the aspects of what that meant at the time; in truth, it had made me feel a little panicky. But now I agreed and could see the grace within it.

Alisa then suggested that I was ready for another guided meditation. "This one will be a bit different, Brienne," she said. "How do you think you'd like a color-therapy session?"

I had never done one before, so I was intrigued. "Sounds great!" I said. Because all these experiences had been so illuminating, I felt sure this one would be, too. As soon as I began meditating, however, I missed the whole color thing because so many other sensations flooded through me. I guess my guides felt there were more important things to share with me.

I actually had my first out-of-body experience. (I respect if you find this too "out there," and I am not going back on my promise to keep it real and not let this book be too New Age-y. But this was an awesome experience that I want to share with you; it's powerful, even if you don't ever experience something like this yourself. Even if you don't ever want to!) At first, I thought I was going to die because I could "see" myself in the room, standing not quite in front but a little to the right of myself. Then I felt my guide, Virginia, come next to me and hold my hand. I physically felt her hand clasp mine. It was intense—that's the only word I can use to describe it. I started to get choked up, but with tears of sheer happiness and joy—greater than I had ever experienced. A single thought flashed through my mind: *I get to go home!* (It was only afterward, as I thought about the experience, that I realized I was not at all concerned about leaving anything here—I was just excited to go "home.")

Virginia sort of chuckled and said, "Oh, no. You have much more work to do here."

Persistent, I asked again if this was my time to go. Again Virginia answered, with as much warmth and love as the first time, "No, it's not your time to go, but if you keep screwing around, it will be." (I still find it funny how our guides talk to us in a way that we can relate to. Virginia, my special guide, swears and says things straight to the point. I love that, because I feel it is only then, when she is talking *my* talk, that I do actually get it.)

Virginia added, "If you think this is beautiful, wait until you see the real stuff. You have no idea! You couldn't handle it now. You'd probably explode or catch on fire."

I then saw an eagle again soaring up on my left side, as if I were looking up in the sky. (I had seen that eagle several times before, and now it was back.) I heard another one of my guides say, "Be still and listen. Listen, because it is not enough that you hear us. You need to listen when we are talking to you. Quit questioning. Pay attention."

I did.

At one point, I was in the middle of a swirling plane of openness. I can't really even describe it. The swirling was slow, not scary like a windstorm or a whirlpool might be if you were in the middle of it. I had never seen this before, and nobody else was there, not even Virginia or my other guides. I thought, *I wonder what this is—this swirling . . . it's so cool. Where am I?*

The next thing I knew, I was cruising down a hallway and could see a door at the end. When I say "cruising", that is exactly what I mean. I was moving *fast* along the right side, as if I had stepped onto a sped-up moving sidewalk. I felt like I was skimming against the wall. I continued along in this way, as if I were gliding fast, not bouncing like what happens when you just walk faster. I was quickly gliding—the sped-up moving sidewalk is the best way to describe it; a force was moving me. I was not moving myself. As I got closer to the door, I started to wonder where it was going to lead me. Just at that moment, I heard Alisa's voice tell me to find a door and open it. I had all but forgotten she was guiding the meditation—or that I even was meditating; it was so surreal. Another thought flashed through my mind: *It's so weird that she said that! I just found a door.*

After the session when we shared what happened, I described the out-of-body experience and the swirling plane. Alisa said that she had experienced things like this herself. I thought it was kind of strange once I was fully conscious, post-meditation. But I guess Alisa was right: Nothing is strange in mediation. Everything just *is*. I was finally trusting—the universe, my guides, and myself. It felt amazing!

Sometime later, a friend asked me about meditating—how I did it, if I had rituals, what I used to begin, that sort of thing. I told her the same things I've said throughout these chapters: that she needed to find what worked for her, just as I had found what worked for me. There are no rules that make meditation work—you don't have to be in a dark room with candles lit and soft music playing, but if that works for you, by all means do that. If you engage your guides, you don't have to worry about how you talk to them—they never judge you, and they never feel that you're bothering them or asking trivial questions. It's okay if you never encounter any guides; whatever manifests is always exactly what we each need. You don't have to recite prayers by rote, or confess your sins, or feel anxious about anything. Just relax; that's what meditation really is: deep relaxation that leads to inner peace, and, even more so, the sense that you are *you* . . . at one with the universe and your higher self.

Over time, I have learned what works best so that I can hear the messages in a crystal-clear way. I still always begin my meditation by focusing on gratitude. Then I simply state, inwardly or out loud, depending upon how I feel in that moment, "Okay, people, show and guide me in a way that I can understand. Show and guide me so I won't freak out. I do not want any energy or thoughts that do not serve me. Okay, let's get down to brass tacks."

I am never disrespectful in the way I speak to and thank my guides, the angels, or the Great Spirit. They are very aware of my personality and understand that I want to cut through the BS and get the show on the road. I found that when I was given too many rapid visions and thoughts, I immediately went straight to my intellect in an attempt to make logical sense of it all. I have always needed to research and believe in things that can somehow be proven by scientific facts and data. However, I was now in a totally different realm, where what I had always done up to that point no longer worked. Not only did I have to let go, I also had to deeply believe. I had to have faith. To put it another way, *thinking* means using the intellect; as soon as you do this, you start to judge the vision and its messages—and yourself.

It takes time to learn how to slow down your thoughts and quiet your mind—it took me a long time. But once you do, you'll be able to observe and witness your thoughts interacting in your life, without judging them . . . and without judging yourself. *Slow down? Are you kidding me?* For a recovering cocaine addict, slowing down feels like being sentenced to live in the DMV. It was torturous to be calm, to wait, to accept, and to arrive at "my turn" without wanting to yell, "What's the problem in here, people?"

But I knew I had to do it, *because* it was so hard, *because* it felt like torture—and because, until I did what I needed to do, I would always feel miserable and incomplete. Again, none of this may work—or even resonate—for you. That's okay. What's *not* okay is denying that you need help or resisting what will help you.

As my process really began to work for me, I experienced amazing results. Instead of flying off the handle emotionally and acting in a way that I would later regret, I now consciously chose how I wanted to react to any given situation. My former habit of getting angry, feeling resentful, and then holding onto that anger and resentment for days was beginning to disappear. Whenever I did get angry, I was able to think to myself, *Okay, why am I getting mad? What's the real reason behind it? I need to witness it for what it is so that I can choose to react in a way that only my beautiful, confident inner goddess would.*

I know that sounds impossible and like a bunch of psychobabble—not to mention conceited!—but I can assure you that it truly changed my life. Let's leave the meditation studio so you'll believe me when I promise to keep it real.

Recently, a longtime girlfriend came to town unannounced. I was so excited to see her that I agreed to make a lunch date that would fit both our schedules, even though I felt a tiny bit irritated that she had not called or e-mailed with a couple of days' notice. Anyway, we found a last-minute time that worked and agreed to meet that afternoon. In the interim, I had a very important conference call that ran into our lunchtime date. I let her know that I was stuck on the call, apologized for not being able to make it, and hoped to see her sometime soon when both our schedules permitted.

I would find out later that, within hours of our missed last-minute lunch, she called my ex-husband in order to accuse me of using drugs, informing him that this was the reason why I hadn't been able to keep our lunch date. When I learned of her behavior, I found it baffling, hurtful, and destructive. Above all, it was a serious false accusation, and I felt that my anger in response to it was completely justified. In addition, not knowing whom to believe—my "friend" or me—my ex was concerned about the kids' time with me. (I would have been, too, if the situation were reversed.) Fortunately, my ex was eventually able to see the situation clearly, and he and I worked through the issue and got past it.

But that did not eliminate the feelings I bore toward someone I had considered to be a good friend of many years' standing. I spun into a state of anger, depression, pain, resentment, and confusion. Why would she, and how could she, treat me like this?

Interestingly, this lesson taught me many valuable things. Prior to that time, I would have sent her a to-the-point e-mail, detailing her ascent to Royal You-Know-What of the Year, and ending our friendship. In my anger and pain, I probably would have said things I didn't really mean and that I would later regret. Here is what I did instead: I immediately sat down and decided to meditate on the whole situation. I asked for clarity on why this was happening and what I should do. And the answers came to me in a very clear and comforting way. I heard my thoughts describe how her actions weren't about me; I had nothing to do with this entire situation, because the problem was hers. This was her unhappiness and judgment blazing at me. These were her personal issues and emotions being unleashed. We all have been there at one time or another. The difference between my pre- and post-awareness reactions was that I had stopped judging. I didn't judge my friend or myself; but I also didn't hold myself responsible for the way she had treated me.

As soon as I did this, I felt good. Instantly I was flooded with happiness, in the truest sense of the word. I immediately thought kind and forgiving thoughts and mentally sent her love to help her resolve her own drama. Then I thought, *Wow! I have never done this before. How fabulous does* this *feel! Great job on balance, awareness, and letting go of judgment.*

At that moment, I felt as if I were officially on my comeback tour, just like a rock star—"Brienne's North American Comeback Tour" or "Brienne's North American Kick-Ass Tour." Yeah! I could sell out arenas and truly rock the house. *This is going to be my best performance yet, because, just like Madonna, I'm reinventing myself, and the reinvented me is going to be even better—because this is the* real *me. And no success is greater than that.*

After that clarity following my friend's actions, I became stronger, physically and mentally, with each passing day. I was standing on my own two feet, completely clean and sober. I had taken an inventory of what I needed to do in order to move on down the road, and I was ready to do just that.

Alisa helped me devise a business plan for how to live my dream of being a writer and artist. The plan included ways to promote my artwork and writing by utilizing social media so that I could connect with others in these fields in order to launch my creative enterprise. This was not a flaky pie-in-the-sky kind of thing; this was a business-minded approach to making my dream a reality, and to earning a living by doing what I loved. I was feeling on top of the world, thinking, *I'm really going to do it. I'm going to do exactly what I've always wanted to do, and that's living a creative, artistic life, developing my writing and painting. This is exciting stuff!* (Remember that it isn't about finding a life coach, or even wanting a life coach. It's about believing in yourself. In the Internet age, resources abound on just about everything. If you put your mind to it, and your heart into it, you can do whatever you want to do. All you need is the faith in yourself and the love for yourself—and then you, too, can live your dream.)

In case you're wondering, yes, this segment of my life was an emotional rollercoaster ride. But, in its wake, I developed a profoundly new outlook on life—and a profoundly improved perspective of myself. I realized that happiness is something that doesn't just happen; rather, happiness is something that evolves and emerges anew as a result of our experiences. All the answers I needed were within, not outside me, as I had previously thought.

Once the business plan was created, I wrote a personal mission statement that would best define my core values, clarity, and focus. (I did this with Alisa's guidance, but if it sounds like something that would work for you, by all means write one on your own.) After taking a personal inventory—which, I warn you, can be a challenging exercise—I was able to come up with what I felt was an honest description of myself. The final aspect of this assignment was to creatively design a sign featuring the statement, and then hang it in a place where I could read it every day. I chose to hang my sign on the bathroom mirror so that I would be able to read it first thing in the morning. Even to this day, I say that statement out loud and with pride: "I am a strong creative force who is connected to mother energy. I am original and smart and constantly growing. I find strength in being *absolutely fabulous.*"

Yes, I do. When I read the last sentence, in particular, I feel great—I put my shoulders back and stand taller. (And, ahem, that's *before* I put on the stilettos!) The simple act of saying the positive affirmation makes me feel as if I can conquer anything. It reminds me to claim my confidence for the day—and to restore my confidence if the prior day had been depleting in any way.

It has taken me years of heartache and bad choices to rediscover my confidence and to gain the wisdom that I am the only one who is going to help me achieve my goals. When I am confident, I am unquestionably solid in my core values, and so I feel no fear and I don't sabotage myself by making bad choices—the inclination toward negative, harmful behavior just evaporates when I feel confident, because I am centered in my own power. This self-confidence also helped me finally find clarity about what job would define me. I had always struggled about how to answer the question, "What do you do for a living?" Now, having put my first foot forward to realize my dreams of being a writer and artist, I could triumphantly answer that question: "What do I do? Why, I'm a writer and artist—that's all I ever wanted to do, and all I was ever meant to do!"

What you think about yourself is much more important than what others think of you.

—M. Annaeus Seneca

8

Out of the Psychic Closet

A Million Sparks of Light

As I continued to move forward in recovery and healing, I felt deeply engaged with, and connected to, the universe—all as a result of living my truth. Yes, life was good. In fact, I couldn't imagine that it could ever get better.

Continuing with my weekly UA tests, I always enjoyed chatting with Kathryn, because she repeatedly gave me insightful advice and encouragement. I continued to find her comments uncanny (in the past, prior to my own discovery of synchronicity at work in my own life, I would have considered them extremely strange). When I say "uncanny," I mean that the things Kathryn said were either exact answers to questions I had asked myself earlier or descriptions of things that had just happened. In either case, she would have had no way of knowing any of it, unless I told it to her, but I had not. As a result, all this validated for me that nothing is random. But I did still wonder. *Why* did I wonder? I can't really answer that. I already believed in synchronicity. Since discovering it, I had been accumulating all the little signs; I dismissed some and completely believed others. Nevertheless, it did still feel very surreal. I had never felt a connection to higher powers, and it all felt a bit awkward. Not that I didn't believe it, because I did; but sometimes I still had to verify that it was actually happening *to me.*

However, the more I explored and the more I trusted what I felt, the more comfortable I became. I accepted the changes I experienced in myself, and as soon as I did that—instead of questioning—it all clicked. As I had done with my relapse and my longtime friend's betrayal, I turned to meditation when I felt confused or doubtful. Whenever I felt that I needed an answer to a question, or that it was time to further contemplate a situation, I meditated and listened to my inner voice.

Coming out of the psychic closet, so to speak, was not exactly the easiest thing to do. Society has placed so many stigmas on the paranormal and its validity. Yes, some of it can be proved by scientific data; however, much of it cannot be. Most of us, including me, resist believing that which cannot be explained logically. I have read, researched, and spoken with many experts in the field in order to gather information to satisfy my questions. You may or may not believe what is said to be currently happening in the universe, and I appreciate that. I absolutely respect others' beliefs, and I know when it's appropriate to share my experiences. As I have become more open to these experiences and beliefs, I have found that some people either are not willing to, or have no desire to, hear about spiritual experiences. Just as I have said from the beginning, everything doesn't resonate with or appeal to everyone else, and that's okay, as long as we respect one another's right to our individual beliefs. My experiences were so thrilling and illuminating that, at first, I wanted to tell *everyone.* I'm telling you all this because we all share the same access to illumination, but it's up to each of us whether we choose to accept that access. I'm not asking you to believe me or to access what I have accessed; I only ask you to respect what I have experienced.

Let me put it all in perspective. Over the course of a few short months (from the point when James introduced me to synchronicity to the point when I discovered my guides during meditation), I had been launched into the metaphysical world. Add to that the fact that, at least initially, I was completely oblivious and clueless as to what it all meant. I trusted it all intuitively, but I didn't really understand it. But the more I experienced, and the more I trusted what I experienced—the more I took on faith, you might say—the more it all fell into place. I say that because, ever since I was a little kid, I had consistently witnessed circumstances that never made sense to me until my newfound connection to the universe. As an adult, I had come to discount the fact that my grandmother, my mom, and I all have always been highly perceptive—sensitive to dreams, intuitive about thoughts and ideas, and even witness to the occasional ghostly sighting. To put it another way, instead of "I had come to discount the fact," I should have said, "I conveniently forgot." I *had* forgotten, and none of this came back to me until I started to meditate. As soon as I found myself, I remembered who I really was—who I always had been, and who I would be forever. All my life, I've had nightmares; my mom has always had, and continues to have, precognitive dreams; my grandmother's experiences were similar. (We've all seen ghosts—more about that later.)

What was happening to me became obvious one day as I sat mulling things over. Recently, I had met a man who was interested in me, but I didn't know why. We were not dating, but I felt like I kept getting mixed thoughts about him, which I couldn't decode. I had just begun to research how to set up a blog when he asked me out for a drink. Sure, one harmless drink (club soda—when I say "harmless," I mean it) should be fine, because he looked kind of like a mellow nerd. During our conversation, he explained that he was a computer expert who knew all about blogs, and he would be happy to help me set up mine.

Aha! Thank you! I just manifested a person to help me with my computer needs. How awesome is that?!

Well, that seemed to be the case; but then again, maybe not. I began to second-guess it all. Quickly. Healing and spirituality are part of a lifelong learning process, and I was still a beginner. The ways in which to request, control, and be grateful for the ability to manifest were still new to me. Very new. Don't get me wrong: I thought it was great that I might have just received a personal computer technician; I just wasn't sure it was safe to trust it at face value. I questioned the safety because I was overlooking the deeper connections behind my request. I had explored this earlier, but I still had trouble integrating it in practical terms. Even now, I still remind myself on a daily basis that these "powers" come not from me but from the Great Spirit, and then they manifest through me to yield the outcome that is best for me and meant for me.

To give you another example, one afternoon I was finishing a mixed-media painting when I thought I would sit and take a break. Again, I started contemplating the computer guy's presence in my life, when all of a sudden I whipped my head around and said, "Who just said that?" I immediately thought, *Oh, my God, did I just think that or did I say it? As in, out loud. Hmmm. Okay, I'm tired. Really tired. I'll just close my eyes and relax.*

I closed my eyes. At first I didn't see anything—well, just what we see when our eyes are closed, the inside of our eyelids. But then that became almost like a screen on which played a crystal-clear "movie," including more images and impressions than I can even recall. Except for the last part. I remember that in detail, because it was an image of the computer guy that clearly explained everything to me. We were kneeling, facing each other with our hands up, palms parallel but not touching. There were vast beams of light between our hands, and I heard a voice. (This was not the voice of one of my guides; it was my own voice, but it didn't sound the same as my regular voice. I surmised that it must have been the voice of my higher self communicating to me.) Anyway, what I heard was that the computer guy was here to inspire me and to share and accumulate energy for later.

Despite my explorations up to this point, that vision jolted me. I opened my eyes, thinking, *What just happened? What did that mean?* That vision was so real that I felt like I was there. I mean, physically there, kneeling face-to-face with this man I barely knew, yet felt utterly comfortable with. Guided meditations were one thing; Alisa led me through those. This was something else entirely—I closed my eyes, and then, without even trying to meditate, had this . . . this *vision.*

Oh, my God, did I fry my brains on all those drugs? Is that what this is?! Am I just screwed up, or am I actually going crazy? No. No. I am not crazy. I'm just tired. But I am not closing my eyes again!

Convincing myself that I was daydreaming, I tried to dismiss it as no big deal. The rest of the day was uneventful, and I went to bed as usual—when I closed my eyes, there were no visions, and I didn't have any dreams that I could remember.

The next morning, however, was quite a different story. I woke up, shot out of bed, and went directly to my easel, where I began to paint in a fury. When I say "in a fury," I mean I was unstoppable, literally. For a day and a half, I cranked out dozens of black-and-white paintings—I worked virtually nonstop. Let me just say that I usually paint in what would be called abstract form. I don't even know how to paint people or anything detailed. During the frenzy, however, I was creating paintings of Renaissance women and angels, nudes, and portraits, as if I had been studying this type of painting for my entire life—and as if I'd had models posing for me. For the record, I have never even taken a serious art class. None of those facts mattered. I simply couldn't stop painting—and I didn't want to, because these paintings just kept coming, pouring out of me, and getting better and better.

Once, when I fell over from sheer physical exhaustion, I started to hear myself talk again: *Oh, no, I'm going crazy. This is it. I am crazy. People get locked up for hearing voices, whether their higher self's voice or otherwise. This is really scaring me.* To add to my confusion, I started to see energy spots. I had no idea what to call them other than "energy spots," because that's exactly what they looked like. Throughout the room, I could see random spots that seemed blurry and sort of wavy, but that were colorless. *Wow,* I thought, *I am definitely going over the edge.* I didn't want to bother Alisa on a day when I wasn't scheduled to see her, so I decided to pack up the smaller images from among those I had just created and drive directly to talk to Kathryn. She made her own schedule at the UA testing facility, and she seemed to know a lot about astrology, tarot, and everything metaphysical—and always enjoyed discussing those topics.

I burst through the door and asked to talk to her in private because I needed her opinion. Even though I was eager to find out what she might know about my recent experience, I was also a little frightened to tell her, in case I *was* going crazy or had been right about drugs frying my brain. But then I realized, *Hey, she has the UA results; she knows I'm not using. Besides, she already sees me pee in a cup—what do I have to hide?* I told her the whole story the same way I've related it here, except that I also showed her every painting and drawing I had brought with me. She listened intently, not saying a word until after I wrapped up the whole thing by asking the most important question of my life: "*What* is happening to me?"

Kathryn laughed out loud. (Thank God she laughed; if she had looked worried, I probably would have had a nervous breakdown on the spot.) It was clear to me in that instant that she knew *exactly* what was happening. She got all excited, gave me a big hug, and exclaimed, "Brienne, congratulations!"

I hugged her back, a little stunned.

Kathryn laughed again, stepping back. "I'm surprised you got 'there' so fast."

Is the whole world in on this joke to drive me to the brink of insanity? I wondered to myself.

Kathryn quickly went on to explain what she meant. "You've discovered your gift. On rare occasions that can come to a person in the form of an 'intuitive breakthrough.'"

Oh, is that all? Well, it's all okay then. That isn't anything like a psychotic break, is it? No. Breakthrough, not break. Hmmm. Maybe I should call Alisa. Maybe I should call Dr. Dani.

I'm sure I must have looked bewildered, because I felt shell-shocked— and I hadn't eaten or slept in almost two days.

Kathryn was unfazed. I think she was almost as excited as I was—maybe more so, because she wasn't half-terrified. She calmly explained what an intuitive breakthrough was, how it took place, and how it worked. "The universe works in a very simple manner," Kathryn said. "I don't want to go into a long explanation of quantum physics, but let's look at what Adam wrote in *The Path of the Dream Healer*. I think he describes it best." She turned toward the bookshelf in her office, located the book she'd just mentioned, and pulled it off the shelf. Opening it, she quickly found what she was looking for and read aloud:

> While there is still much we don't know about our universe, the most important concept to understand about the origin of the universe is that everything is interconnected. If you were able to freeze time just prior to the Big Bang, you would see that for an instant only one common energy—one singularity—existed. Everything in the universe shares a connection to everything else. The result is our web of interconnectedness. This interconnectedness explains your fundamental ability to influence your life, and consequently, your health.

"Do you understand, Brienne?" Kathryn asked after she'd finished reading. "This is all about the power of manifestation and synchronicity. The same things we've been talking about for months. They're already in motion for you. They've been active in your life for quite some time, I think. You just didn't recognize it. You weren't ready to see it—or to trust it."

"I am now, though." I beamed at my friend.

"I know you are." Kathryn put the book down on her desk, and we hugged again. "Here, take this home and read it." She pressed the book into my hand.

"Thanks—for the book, and for, well, for everything, Kathryn."

She smiled, and we said goodbye. I took the book and my paintings and drawings and went home. After reading the book cover to cover, I felt secure that the explanation for the visions I saw and the voices I heard fell under the category of *intuition*. Quite simply, I was opening to mine—even more so than I had been up to now. I agree with Kathryn that Adam explains it best:

We all have access to the same information. An infinite amount of information is passing through you at any given time. Your brain acts as the filtering mechanism by constantly selecting the information that it determines relevant. . . . Some people are more skilled than others at focusing their connection to this information field; they are said to have psychic, telepathic, or telekinetic capabilities. We all possess these capacities, which can be developed further with practice.

I wasn't going insane; I had just opened to my psychic abilities! Does "becoming a psychic" mean I have to start wearing loose, draped tops and long flowing skirts and European-style walking sandals and head wraps? I hope not. I have a fitted sweater that I adore, because it makes my boobs look awesome. I'm not going to repeat how I feel about my tight jeans and my stilettos. And I'm sorry, but my hair is *way* too fantastic for me to even consider wearing a turban.

The next thing that went through my mind was, *How in the world am I going to tell my parents? Should I invite them out to dinner and just lay it all on the line?* "Hey, Mom and Dad. Um. Guess what? Turns out, I'm psychic!" I could not imagine that going down too easily over a basket of chips and salsa at El Toro. But, then again, my mom and grandma are psychic, too, whether they know it or not, so . . .

Always remember who you are, and why you are here.
—Caroline Adams

Six Degrees of Separation, Universe-Style

We each have to find our own way, and the journey of finding ourselves—like the journey of life, regardless of which path we each pursue—is made up of moments that are sad, happy, funny, beautiful, ugly, scary, amazing, magical, and on and on in their variety.

Remember, it is not about reaching a final destination; it is about *getting there*. It is about the quality of the getting there. Getting there means *living*. Living well, and living true to yourself.

Over the course of the two days that followed my painting frenzy, I tried to digest all the new information I'd received, planning with whom to share it and what to reveal. I did realize that I had opened up to this information because there was a sense of urgency as to my using it in my

108

life—but don't ask me how or why I thought that. Once again, I had no clue how I knew; I just *knew*.

I turned to Alisa for guidance, because she had experience in energy healing, shamanism, and spiritual connection, as well as a huge library of informational books that could help me. Again, it was no mistake that I had chosen Alisa to be my life coach, because she had become a great source of strength and inspiration. Indeed, she was my earthly guide and mentor in many ways. I had originally thought I was going to see Alisa in order to find a job; I guess I did, in a way. It just wasn't exactly the job or career that I'd had in mind.

All of which proves that what we need and most deeply desire finds a way to manifest; all we need to do is open to the universe and then get out of the way. The last part is often the hardest. Self-sabotage—getting in our own way—is the most hurtful thing we can do to ourselves, and we've all done it at least once in our lifetime. (If you've done it only once, you're very lucky—and very wise!) In any case, "psychic" and "latent artistic genius" are not typical career fields that one can check off when completing a career-interest questionnaire; even checking the vague "other" could be awkward at explanation time. "Well . . . yes, after rehab I discovered this artistic talent I never knew I had. All of a sudden I began 'channeling' Botticelli. Then I started hearing voices. *That's* how I knew I was psychic, too." *Hmmm . . . maybe not.*

I mentioned all this to Alisa when I arrived at her studio.

"Living with your gifts isn't always going to be easy, Brienne," she said. "Life is about balance. Without sadness, you can't fully appreciate joy; without struggle, you can't fully appreciate bliss. Living your truth is bliss, but that doesn't mean you won't have moments of struggle within it."

I thanked her, took the books she recommended, and left. As I drove home, I thought about what she'd said. It made a lot of sense, but I knew I would have to ponder it a while before it all sank in. I could hardly wait to meditate on it later.

The day after I saw Alisa, I went to meet with Dr. Dani, just to validate that, indeed, I was not going crazy. (Trust and faith are good and important, but you can't be too careful. I had to make sure I was okay, not just for my own peace of mind, but, even more so, for my kids' sake.)

Dr. Dani listened intently as I related all that had happened, right up through Alisa's comments from the day before. "I can tell you that what you've been experiencing really is not all that uncommon, Brienne," she said.

Whew! I breathed an audible sigh of relief. Those comments, from a trained therapist whom I trusted and respected, not only validated my experiences but also brought me vast relief. Now I could enjoy being a magnificent psychic *sans* turban, without the sneaky fear that I might be a total nut job. Awesome!

Dr. Dani smiled slightly when she heard me sigh. "How do you feel about it all?"

"Good," I hedged. "Better, now that I know I'm not going nuts."

Her smile deepened. "I suppose you would. Not all that long ago, psychic gifts and insanity were not separated. We've come a long way. It takes courage to open up to and accept our gifts."

Were psychology and metaphysics linked? Alisa, Dr. Dani, and Kathryn all were telling me basically the same thing. I would need to meditate on that, too.

Dr. Dani continued, "The year 2012 is approaching, you know."

What? What does that *mean?* "Um . . . I guess so . . . yeah," I mumbled.

"The ancient Mayan civilization predicted that the year 2012 would mark either the end or the beginning of human awakening."

I nodded. I had never heard of that before, but I was fascinated. Dr. Dani went on to point out a number of current examples of awakening that occurred in everyday life. "People are awakening to universal intuitiveness, Brienne. Think of the increased interest in metaphysics—TV, movies, and books. People are seeking answers, and they want to learn all the secrets. More than that, people are becoming open to the ideas that govern the universe."

I nodded. "They're accessing synchronicity, without even understanding its magnitude."

"I agree," Dr. Dani said, soon indicating that our time was up for that session.

I pondered some more as I drove home. *Am I going to have one amazing meditation after all of this, or what!* Then I thought about synchronicity, and it hit me: Why is the game Six Degrees of Separation to Kevin Bacon so popular? Seriously, that guy is everywhere. Don't take my word for it, play the game—he and just about everyone else in the world has had some sort of connection to one other.

That's synchronicity.

When opportunity knocks, open the door—even if you're in your bathrobe.

—Heather Zshock

Buying a Lottery Ticket—I Mean, Throwing a Tarot Card

Not everyone discovers their true self (higher self) by doing bikram yoga or looking through a crystal. Not everyone has their natal chart prepared or tarot cards thrown. Some people swear by these things; others run from them like the plague. And it's okay, either way. We can find the answer to the mysteries of the universe in the rush of the ocean or at the top of a mountain or in the stillness of the desert as easily as we can find them around the dinner table or at the mall or in the garden. We can find them with our families, friends, and significant others, as well as with the strangers we meet in passing but cannot forget. All it's about is being open and aware—and paying attention.

I should clarify exactly what my newfound "psychic abilities" meant. I didn't fully understand it all at first, as I have already shared. As I delved into the research materials in order to determine what lay in store for me, I was astounded—not just by the topic itself, although it is fascinating, but by the amount of materials available on the topic. Dozens upon dozens of books are dedicated to psychic abilities, and although I have not read all of them, I feel that I have read enough to be able to say that they relay this same basic message: There are several types of psychic abilities, and people can possess just one or a combination of them.

To use myself as an example, the gifts I have accessed do not fall under the psychic ability of predicting the future, which is what most people think *psychic* means. That means that if I bought a lottery ticket, I could not predict whether I would win or not. Damn! My gift is one of a more intuitive nature. It is specifically known as *clairvoyance,* which means that, although I cannot predict the future, I have a very clear understanding of the present (the word actually means "clear sight"). So, I am clear as to what is happening in the present time, but that may or may not be related to my personal life. Furthermore, the term *clairvoyance* has several subcategories, which determine how one comes to know which type he or she has. Essentially, intuition is the sixth sense (the other five are sight, sound, smell, taste, and touch). In terms of informational senses, we know, hear, see, feel, and intuit. My intuitive sense is strong, as are my seeing and hearing senses—all of which explains how I knew things without knowing how I knew, and how I had visions and heard voices.

Life is definitely a journey. I felt like I needed a seatbelt for mine.

> *Live in each season as it passes; breathe the air, drink the drink, taste the fruit.*
>
> **—Henry David Thoreau**

All in a Day's Work

Faith is a wonderful thing, but most humans need something concrete to believe in, even if whatever that is, is a symbol of faith. "Send me a sign," people pray, time and time again. That's all well and good, and perfectly understandable, but the sign isn't always concrete, either. More often than not, it isn't. Faith, like intuition, is felt; either one believes, or one does not believe. There are no guarantees, and there is no proof, per se.

I knew this—or, I should say, I intuited this—but I still searched for proof. Seek, and you shall find.

As I struggled to understand and accept what was happening to me, I kept asking out loud, "Show me something—anything—that will prove this in my day-to-day life."

The first sign was another verbal confirmation from Alisa that what I felt was completely normal.

I went to see her one afternoon and described how I was still struggling.

"It's perfectly normal, Brienne," Alisa assured me. "You're integrating a new belief system. It takes time."

I nodded, but she could tell I was not really okay with it.

"I have an idea," she continued. "There's metaphysical store I recommend. You can go there to pick up some things that will help protect your soul, thoughts, and house. I think that might help you feel more comfortable."

I wrote down the items Alisa described—a sort of metaphysical grocery list—said goodbye to her, and then followed the directions she'd given me to get to the store.

As soon as I stepped inside, I felt overwhelmed. Where to begin? This place was packed with all sorts of intriguing items, but I had no idea what most of them were. A few feet from the door was a display with some pretty bottles of oil. *Nice air fresheners,* I thought.

Just then an older lady appeared from out of nowhere. "Welcome!" she chirped. The wind chimes above the door were still tinkling slightly from my arrival, but I'd been browsing for a few moments. *Where did she come from? Maybe she's psychic . . . she does work here. Oh, lighten up. She seems pleasant enough.*

"I see you've found our special oils," she said. I couldn't tell if she was reading my thoughts, but something about the way she'd said "special oils" gave me pause. *Okay. I have a feeling these are not air fresheners, after all.*

She went on to explain, in the kindest tone of voice, the true purpose of these oils: One swishes them around in the mouth, without swallowing the oil, and then blows into the air to get rid of "entities." *Hmmm. Well . . . I don't think* that's *what I need.* I was pretty sure that I was definitely in the wrong place, with the wrong grocery list.

"I'm . . . um . . . kind of new at this. A friend suggested I come here."

She kept smiling; waves of kindness and calm just emanated from this woman. She was tiny, but I had the impression that she was enormously strong—I have no idea how I knew that. Clairvoyance, I guess.

In spite of my initial concerns, I grew comfortable in her presence and read off the list of items that Alisa had recommended. "Would you mind pointing me in the right direction?"

"Follow me." She led me toward the section where they kept the candles and then explained the different kinds they had.

Pointing to two types of candles, I said, "Great! I'll take one of each of these, because I've got some unusual business going on right now." I smiled. "I appreciate your help."

She had not stopped smiling since first coming over to me. "You said 'unusual business,'" she said.

I nodded.

"What kind of unusual business? I might be able to help."

At that, I *did* feel uncomfortable again—not because of her, but at the idea that someone else might be able to hear. In a store like that, it probably wouldn't even raise an eyebrow, but still. After looking over both shoulders to make sure no one was in earshot, I leaned in and said quietly, "Well, I've been seeing and hearing things. And manifesting things, within minutes of asking."

I had barely finished the sentence when she lit up, exclaiming, "Oh, honey! Congratulations! How exciting for you. Oh, my, this is so magical!"

She reached up and put both hands on my shoulders. Her smile had expanded into a beam of radiant joy.

Sure. Mm-hmmm. This is so magical and exciting that I can hardly stand it. No concerns whatsoever that I might be—I don't know—nuts?!?! Kathryn, Alisa, and even Dr. Dani had validated that I was okay, but I was still the one who had to live through it. Sometimes it did feel magical and exciting, but other times it just felt weird. Nevertheless, I forced a smile, even though I wasn't quite sure what to make of it all. I could not deny the calming effect that this woman had on me. In spite of my reservations, I relaxed again; I just felt comfortable in her presence, plain and simple. *If I trust her, it's for a reason. I've already come this far.*

Sensing my ambivalence, she proceeded to explain the basic concepts of what was happening to me.

I nodded in response to all of it, which gibed with what both Kathryn and Alisa had said.

Then she said, "I read tarot cards here, you know. Would you like me to read yours?"

Why not? This day could not possibly get any stranger. I'd had cards thrown before, and although I didn't really want to revisit that painful time, the wisdom had been right on the money.

I agreed, and she took me over to her table and shuffled the deck. "All right now. Choose your cards and place them face down on the table."

I did what she said. When I finished, she slowly turned each card over and studied it carefully for her reading. She didn't speak until she had turned over the fourth card, and then she said, "Oh, this doesn't surprise me: You are profoundly clairvoyant."

My stomach did a little flip, because I realized I had physically manifested the confirmation I'd asked for. Undoubtedly this was the second confirmation presenting itself in one day. "Really?" I asked.

"Oh, my, yes. This card confirms it." She held it out toward me.

No kidding. Okay, you have my attention now. I am open to listening and learning.

We both agreed that, from the moment our eyes had met in the shop, we felt a connection. She described it as "a lifelong knowledge of having spent time together"—for me it was more like what I'd described earlier, just that I felt comfortable in her presence. Both descriptions could be termed an *unexplained connection*, as in, synchronicity. I was beginning to feel a little unsettled about the whole afternoon, particularly because I was experiencing this kind of *déjà vu* feeling, and I couldn't figure out why. As we talked after the reading, we discovered that the woman used to work at my chiropractor's office—so we *had* met previously in this lifetime.

Chuckling to myself, I thought, *So much for my psychic abilities!* But I was more than relieved, because it made me feel that I hadn't gone completely over the edge.

"Oh, you are still deeply psychic, dear," my new friend assured me. *Hmmm. Maybe. She sure is—I hadn't said aloud a word of what I'd been thinking.*

We said goodbye, and I promised to visit again soon.

That's not all of it, though. Not by a long shot. The icing on my psychic cupcake was not to happen until the evening of that same day.

Kathryn had previously attended a few local psychics' meetings that included tarot reading and storytelling. She asked me to join her, and I thought, *How perfect is this? I can ask somebody what to do about my newfound ability and then see how it fits with today's experience.*

I briefly explained my afternoon encounter to Kathryn as we sat eating pie at the local truck-stop diner where the meeting was to take place. I was still in a state of disbelief over all that had happened to me—all that continued to happen to me—and so the idea of meeting a psychic group at a diner seemed not one bit surprising.

Upon arriving at the meeting/reading, each person put his or her energy on an item, placed it in an envelope marked only with his or her birth date, and then put the envelope on a mounting pile. The item could be anything—a picture, a rock, a ring—any object that pertained to whatever the person wanted clarity on. Following Kathryn's instructions as to what to bring, I had brought a picture of myself with my two kids, sealed it in the envelope with my birth date labeled on it, and dropped it on the pile of envelopes.

One by one, each of the six readers stood up, picked up an envelope, and then described any feelings or words that he or she received from that envelope. After the second person read, I turned to Kathryn and said, "See that guy down there? He has my envelope, and he will stand up out of order and read mine." I followed that statement with, "Oh, God, if that happens I am going to trip out."

Sure enough, a few minutes later the guy I had pointed out stood up and read my envelope. He said he could see a major personal transformation for me and that I was incredibly psychic.

I calmly turned to Kathryn and said, "See? See what I mean? This is beyond understanding."

Throughout the meeting, my head had been hurting. I was now in the throes of headache agony. I bent over in my chair and rubbed my temples. A very nice older lady sitting next to me asked me if I was feeling okay. *No, hardly. I'm feeling anything* but *okay.*

Up until that moment, I had been very cautious about sharing the feelings I was currently experiencing. I did feel somewhat comfortable at this meeting, but not completely. There was something about the nice older lady sitting next to me, though. Kind of like what I'd experienced earlier that day in the store, but more intense. The woman sitting next to me struck me as incredibly wise. She was also lovely, and she exuded peacefulness—even more so than the woman in the store had; that woman had been calm, whereas this woman was filled with serenity . . . an inner peace much deeper than just being calm. It was similar but not the same. The lady next to me was plump, with long, wavy gray hair. Her bright blue eyes were almost dimmed by the beam of her joyous smile. I instantly envisioned her wearing a long velvet dress and carrying a tall, gnarled wooden walking staff. If she had emerged from the woods and proclaimed her royalty among the forest fairies, I would have believed her.

Without further prompting, I began telling her about my recent episodes. I explained that I thought my headache was caused, in part, by the fact that I was completely confused as to what I was supposed to do with this newfound ability. Her beaming smile broadened. "Oh, darling, I can answer that for you. You are a healer. You are a lightworker, and you don't even know it. Why, a hundred years ago you would have been burned at the stake."

Fantastic news! One more solid validation that I was, indeed, exactly where I was supposed to be. Teensy point of dismay, however: I could have done without the burned-at-the-stake part.

By the end of the meeting, my headache was so intense, I thought my head might explode. Not only did my head hurt, but my entire body ached, too. I said goodbye to the lady I'd met and to Kathryn, drove straight home, and went right to bed, where I slept for twelve hours. I think my mind and body just shut down from information overload; it felt like I had just survived the longest day of my life.

When I woke up the next morning, I felt a bit lighter and more energetic. I was generally excited to see what would unfold for me during the day. It seemed that, on a daily basis, I was experiencing more validations that my spirituality was guiding me, instead of my trying—unsuccessfully—to control it. The fears and uncertainties were beginning to fall away as I gained more strength in awareness.

I began to experience an inner shift that made me grateful for everything I had experienced, even the most emotionally devastating parts. It felt a little surreal to be *thankful* for all my pain and suffering, but they had lifted the fog. I realized that it was this very same lifting that allowed me to truly learn the lessons from my experiences so that I could find the way to navigate my life. I can tell you for certain that the year before I definitely would *not* have been saying thank you to anyone, let alone myself, for all the pain and suffering I had endured.

Everything happens for a reason.

> *Your love is a strong force. It lightens that which presumes to weigh you down.*
>
> **—Sophia Bedford-Pierce**

9

Call to Duty

From Darkness to Bright Light

I kept telling myself, "Life is a journey. One day at a time, one step at a time." That is easier said than done. No matter how much I coached myself, part of me still wanted to scream, "Are we there yet? C'mon already—can't we just get there?!" But the deeper part of me knew that there is no "there," per se. That's why we all feel, at one time or another—no matter how evolved we become—that we aren't there yet. We can't get there—all we can do is just *be*. To put it another way, I had emerged from a very dark place and was embracing the light. That takes courage—if I may say so—and faith and trust and hope and love. A pretty tall order. Adjusting from darkness to bright light is a big deal. I decided to just keep trusting my intuition. As I practiced what I was learning, I realized that adjusting, too, takes time. When we're in the dark, we can flip a switch to turn the light on; but, until our eyes adjust, we're going to squint. That is just a natural reflex.

I told myself it was okay to squint for as long as I needed to—what was not okay was running back into the dark.

Some days I needed to squint more than others, and I was okay with that. I also firmly believed that knowledge is power, so I began soaking up every bit of information I could get on the subject of metaphysics and psychic abilities. In doing so, I came across a particular author who is a recognized expert in the field, and who has published multiple books devoted to her own experiences: Doreen Virtue, PhD. Dr. Virtue's background appealed to me because not only is she well versed on the subject, she is also psychic herself. Her numerous books detail her extensive knowledge and familiarity with angelic, elemental, intuitive, and ascended-master realms. (Again, I am not going back on my promise that this is not a New Age-y book. It really isn't. Not completely, anyway. It's about all my experiences, and these are just too much a part of me to leave out. It would be like writing about myself and not mentioning my stilettos. I mean, c'mon. Let's be real.)

Anyway, during my research, I came across Dr. Virtue's book *The Lightworker's Way: Awakening Your Spiritual Power to Know and Heal.* The title immediately resonated. *This is* exactly *what I have been looking for! Thank you for sending me the title via the synchronicity of an obscure e-mail.* Once again, I was receiving the answer to my plea for help in understanding what to do with my new gifts. I had checked my e-mail inbox a few moments before and discovered a completely random e-mail from an advertiser that I would have normally marked as SPAM and not opened—that is, if my spam filter didn't catch it. I guess the universe is not deterred by cyber safety. In any case, I kind of thought, *Hmmm . . . what's this?* But I was curious, so I trusted my intuition that it felt interesting, and I opened the e-mail. What do you know! In that "obscure" and "random" e-mail was an advertisement for the Dr. Virtue title I mentioned.

To cut to the chase, I ordered the book to be shipped overnight, as I could hardly wait to dive into it. When it arrived, I tore open the packaging, took out the book, and curled up on the sofa to begin reading immediately. It didn't take more than two pages of reading for me to know without a doubt that this was a book I was meant to read. On page two of the preface, Dr. Virtue provided a checklist to help the reader determine if he or she might be a lightworker. A lightworker: feels called to heal others; has had mystical experiences (psychic premonitions, angelic encounters, etc.); has endured harsh life experiences that eroded the knowledge of his or her divine perfection; seeks to heal the self as a first step toward healing the world; feels compelled to teach, write, or counsel others about these experiences, using him- or herself as a model; feels assured of having a higher purpose in this lifetime, even if unsure of exactly what it is and/or how to pursue it. *Wow!* As in, *Oh, my God.* As I read down the checklist, I felt myself agreeing with almost every statement. *That's me. Yup,. me again.* And so forth. I knew this book would lead me to a new understanding of and appreciation for my gifts—and how to accept and use them without feeling like I was losing my mind. *This is it!* I thought. *Right here on this page is clear validation! The universe is instructing me to follow what I feel is my calling—what I* know *is my calling. Yes! I can, and I will.* At the core of my being, I knew I was revitalizing a long-lost dream, even though I had awakened to these gifts only very recently. *I can't believe I feel this way after reading only two pages! How am I going to feel when I finish the book? How awesome is this?! I have to just keep reading.*

Being the type of person who always wants to take a shortcut or find an easy answer—remember my description of feeling like I was trapped in the DMV—I was hoping that Dr. Virtue's book was going to be a kind of how-to manual for budding psychics. Complete outline, easy-to-follow steps, everything I could possibly need to fulfill all the feelings she included in the checklist—possibly even a list of publisher names and phone numbers, so that when I finished my own book, I'd know exactly whom to call. Um . . . well, not exactly.

One of my lessons in life has been to realize that taking shortcuts does not allow the process—including the enjoyment of the process—to happen. What I read resonated because of what I was already experiencing, as well as what I still needed to experience, in order to fully engage in the process. *Hello-o-o-o! Any of this sound familiar? It's about the process, not the outcome. It's about the journey, the path—getting there, not being there, because there is no "there," remember?* It clicked for me in that instant: The outcome is the "there" that doesn't really exist; or that is, at best, illusive. The process is the path, and savoring every step, whether painful or joyful, is the only way to truly be alive. Another aha moment.

What Dr. Virtue really meant was that, in order to publish my book, I had to first believe in myself, then trust the guidance of the Great Spirit, and finally know that, in fact, I do create my own reality. In other words, if I were to write and publish a book, I would have to be the person to get me there. Or, as Dr. Virtue put it, "If you hold on to your faith and dreams, anything you see will eventually become a physical reality. However, if your faith wavers or your dreams constantly flit from one image to another, your reality will reflect this fear and confusion."

> *Desire to have things done quickly prevents their being done thoroughly.*
>
> **—Confucius**

Employee of the Month

One of the best things about self-employment is that you are absolutely certain that the winner of Employee of the Month will deserve the honor, because it will be you! Plus, the weekly staff meetings are always productive and brilliantly run. Okay, okay—yes, I'm being facetious. But it's serious, too. Part of accepting that you have found your true path and are living your truth every day is that you *are* employee of the year, month, week, day, hour, minute, and second—because you are the star of your own life. That is another aspect of coming out of the darkness and into the light—out of storms and into fair weather—there is nothing more exhilarating than seeing the sun after days on end of rain and clouds. There are many silver linings to be found in the dark clouds of the hardships and pain that we all encounter as an inevitable part of life. The trick is remembering that these are things that manifest in our lives so that we can learn and grow; but whether we learn and grow, and how much we learn and grow, is up to each of us.

We can ignore our silver linings, or we can make our own if we don't see any shimmering in the gathering clouds. Either way, life is what we choose to make it.

As I've described, accepting my newfound talents was extremely hard to handle at first, to say the least. A big part of it was that I still worried about what people would think. For instance, what was I going to tell my friends when they inquired what I had been up to lately? *Um, let's see: I just had my nails done, went out to dinner with a friend, and saw a few ghosts/spirits along the way. While at dinner, "someone" whispered the name of my friend's father in my ear. I went home and found a family of spirits standing in my kitchen. Pretty typical, don't you think? Not!!*

At that point, I had already read Dr. Virtue's book cover to cover, which led me to do further research on many aspects of metaphysics. I spent every spare moment learning, reading, and studying. Part of my struggle stemmed from the fact that I was, literally, caught between two different worlds. I was physically living on the same earth where I'd lived up to that point, of course; but on an emotional and spiritual level, the topics I was delving into beckoned to me to reach out to someplace farther and deeper than this earthly plane. It was like I was here, but my soul was traveling much of the time. Frequently I felt torn—not wanting to leave this world (by that I mean join an ashram or move to a psychic commune), but also feeling like I didn't completely belong here anymore, because the call of the otherworld was so strong and affected me so deeply.

The intuitive feelings and overall sense of peace and clarity that I had discovered during the course of my journey enthralled me. During meditation, especially when I accessed my guides, I felt a sense of peace that was so complete, it defies describing in words. I was completely comfortable with all of this; better than that, I loved and embraced it. What I didn't understand—and feared, to be honest—were the random ghostlike appearances of people, sometimes alone and other times in groups that appeared to be families, making themselves known to me. It was, well, creepy. To back up for a second, yes, I did describe them as "random," and I know nothing is random, so my thinking of these experiences in that way should have been a signal that I was resisting, but I didn't get the signal. I didn't get it because, as I said, it was creepy. It completely freaked me out, more often than not. Adjusting to being psychic can be as weird at first as adjusting to anything else. It wasn't like I could just say, "Well, I know I'm psychic, so there's nothing to worry about. I'll just beam cosmic love to the creepy energy that is totally freaking me out, and it will be okay. This is awesome!" Maybe it's like that for some newbies, but it sure wasn't for me. And that's okay. What matters is that I was as honest as I could be about how my experiences made me feel. I knew that, no matter what else I did or didn't do, honesty was my primary responsibility—forever.

So, I tried to stay calm and just be with my feelings, waiting to see what happened, because all this was a process and a journey—my process and my journey. I was okay. Okay-ish. The problem was seeing the spirits. The more frequently I saw them, the more frightened I became. Here's a visual: One minute I'm watching TV and minding my own business, and the next I turn around to see a mother, father, and young child dressed in turn-of-the-last-century farm clothes. I mean, really. C'mon. It's not like I said out loud or thought inwardly, "Oh, Farmer Jones! How about you, your wife, and junior stopping by for tea?" It was freakin' scary! And that's all there is to it. Plus, it wasn't a gradual fade-in or a hazy blur—the farm-family image was like all the others, instantaneous and crystal clear, alarmingly sharp in its detail, as if real people were standing in my living room. Now that you have the visual, let me just say that the instant image of the farm family was enough for me to shut off everything—all the feelings of sensitivity, openness, and trust that I had worked so hard to bring forth . . . that I had accepted, embraced, and eventually grown to love. I still loved those feelings, but I was overwhelmed by my fear. When fear is overwhelming, it can cloud our judgment, negate positive energy, and paralyze us. I had no idea what these spirits were or what they wanted from me, and because I was so overwhelmed by my fear, it didn't even occur to me to ask or to meditate.

I had kind of shrunk into the fear, but I had not stopped my research, and I hadn't given up on my new way of living in truth. Basically I focused on staying aware, but inwardly I prayed that I would not see anything else scary. A day or so after the farm-family visit, I was working at my computer, again minding my own business. All of a sudden and for no apparent reason, I instantly and unequivocally felt like a "scary person" was in the other room. There is no other way to describe why or how I came to feel this; I just did. I felt that deep, knot-in-the-gut kind of fear like when I was a little kid feeling convinced that monsters were under my bed, waiting to eat me as soon as my mother turned out the light and walked down the hall. This fear was that irrational, but also that unrelenting, and that real—so much so that I wouldn't go into the other room. That presence had enough power to frighten me into not wanting to even move an inch out of my chair for fear I might see something. It was like being a prisoner in my own house. Telling myself I was being ridiculous was to no purpose.

As I became more exhausted by these feelings and sightings, I made an appointment to see Alisa to talk over what was happening. How she described it made perfect sense, as usual.

"I'm not discounting what you're feeling, Brienne," she told me. "Try not to worry about it. It isn't personal. It's as simple as this: When you become more 'enlightened,' you begin to radiate pure love and light, and the darkness becomes attracted to it."

"Okay," I said, still feeling miserable, confused, and afraid.

Alisa picked up on my energy. "It's kind of like a bug zapper. What happens when you turn the light on?"

"The nasty mosquitoes are drawn to the light," I replied, still not completely sure where she was going with this. I really hate bugs, so how this image was going to help was not exactly clear to me.

"Exactly!" Alisa clapped her hands together. "The bug flies toward the light—*zap!*—the white light eliminates the bug. Right?"

"Right!" Now I was getting it. "Dark forces are attracted to my light, and so I have to zap them." Visions of myself in beyond-awesome superhero outfits took shape. The dark forces were no match for me.

"Don't go too crazy with the images," Alisa laughed. "It was just an example. Essentially, when you become stronger, the dark forces also become stronger and seek to 'knock your light out'—not just to destroy you, but also to ensure their own continuance. To do this, they use fear. So, just don't let them make you feel afraid. They can't hurt you. You're strong enough to fight them."

Okay, so maybe I didn't need the costume (mildly disappointing, because I'd look awesome in it, especially the stiletto-heeled knee boots I'd been mentally designing), but I was going to walk the walk and talk the talk. Big time. As soon as Alisa explained it, I realized that this was exactly what had been happening to me, but it was about to end. As in, *right now.*

I took the reins and brought the fear wagon to a screeching halt. Fright night was over—at my house or anywhere else around me. I went home and stated out loud in a firm voice, "To every dark thing or force that might come my way, you are not welcome, so don't even bother." As soon as I'd said the words, I felt enormously relieved, as if a two-ton brick had been lifted from my shoulders. Ever since then, those dark and scary forces have not shown up.

Even so, I still felt as if I were on a colossal rollercoaster of emotions, and I was getting physically wiped out. I wasn't afraid anymore, but I still had a lot to learn about protecting my own energy and not letting other things drain and affect me. The truth is, I was beginning to fall apart, because the more in touch I became with my own openness, the more I was flooded. I could, literally, feel other people's emotions—as in, physically feel another person's pain, happiness, anger, and whatever else that individual was experiencing at that moment.

This was a very intense time; so much so that, a couple of times, I begged my higher guides to not make me do this job anymore. It was just becoming too painful, and I had a hard time separating my emotions from those of others. Despite my research, this was all new territory for me; my head hurt constantly, and I was starting to feel physically ill. But I knew I had to press on.

In the midst of reading every book and article I could get my hands on, I came across something that seemed to fit my situation perfectly. Sherrie Dillard's *Discover Your Psychic Type* put into words exactly the way I felt:

> It often happens that people who have no interest in psychic
> or intuitive phenomena find themselves in the midst of an

otherworldly experience they cannot explain. . . . Suddenly they find themselves involved in an extraordinary situation that has no reasonable explanation. They may not want it or be looking for it. They may not believe it.

Yes, that's it. That's me exactly! There I was, minding my own business, and then some ghosts decided to show up at my place and turn my world upside down.

Again, I felt relieved; and I still felt determined to just keep traveling my path, but something was missing. Then I had a turning point. Both Dr. Dani and Alisa were drilling the same thing into my head: If this was the path I was to follow (or career I was to pursue), then I had better stand tall and own it. I continued to struggle with the issue of having always felt like a failure because I had not accomplished anything nearly as great as my friends and family around me. Failure had always been a sensitive spot with me; I still persisted in believing that others' recognition of me would make my life fantastic.

One day I realized that time was up. I did have to stand tall and own who I was and what I wanted, confident that no one else's opinion mattered but mine. It wasn't until I did that—actually owned that I am who I am, and I'm completely happy and satisfied with who that is—that my struggle stopped. It's true that I may not have awards, titles, paychecks, or newspaper articles to validate and praise me, but it's equally true that I have discovered that I never needed them in the first place. As soon as I made that discovery and really owned and believed it, I felt comfortable in my own skin—*finally.* That, in turn, made it easier to continue owning who I was and how I lived. I was then able to stand tall, with my head held high, knowing I could look everyone I met straight in the eye, comfortable with meeting him or her, because I was proud to be me. I don't mean that in an arrogant way; I am not talking about walking with a swagger or an attitude that is in any way obnoxious or demeaning toward others. By "standing tall," I mean that I know who I am, where I've been, and where I am going—and I don't care what anyone else thinks of me. (That is not the same as not caring about other people and not caring about their opinions; it just means not letting others' opinions of you be more important than your opinion of you.)

Self-confidence is a priceless commodity that cannot be bought or faked, and only you can give it to yourself. It seems to come easily to those who use it and don't abuse it, and once cultivated, it should be treasured.

No one can make you feel inferior without your consent.
—Eleanor Roosevelt

Stand Tall—Walk Proud

We are who we are, and we live through what we live through; at some point on our souls' journey, we must accept and embrace all this. We must, because we don't have a choice.

At the end of the day, the only person you can be sure will stick around for your entire lifetime is you. In other words, you can really rely only on you. So, stand tall, walk proud, and own it. Own *all* of it. No one else can get through what you get through, because no one else is you. There's nothing wrong with being proud of that. Better yet, there's everything *right* with being proud of that, and if you're not, there's nothing else worth being proud of.

It had never occurred to me that I was harboring fear and resentment about the custody arrangement my ex and I had agreed upon for our children. That is, until one afternoon when I realized just how large a load I'd been carrying on that score. A single instant made it all crystal clear, knocking me for a loop.

I was out with my brother, and he started talking about a mutual friend. "She doesn't have custody of her two kids, you know," he said.

"I know." A pit formed in my stomach; I felt it churn and then knot.

"In the state of Washington, if the mom loses custody of the kids, she must be really messed up."

I didn't respond. It's true my children do not live with me. My brother's offhand judgments of this woman we both knew forced me to realize that people were probably thinking much the same about me. I was devastated. All I could do was sit there, horrified, as I listened to him wax on, spouting one judgment after another about someone else's battle, which he knew nothing about.

I honestly cannot remember the rest of what he said. But, in that instant, I realized beyond a shadow of a doubt that I had been trying to ignore—or deny—that people were likely judging me in the same manner, concluding the same things about me, assessing me personally based on what they decided they "knew" about me. I already said I was devastated; I was outraged, too, because that judgment was so wrong and so unfair . . . but the judgment of others usually is. I knew that was part of life. I had come so far. But there was something about being judged as a less-than-good mother that I couldn't handle. That judgment ripped through the core of my being like a knife twisting in my heart. At the same time, however, it was another turning point for me: I was not going to carry this burden—not only because it would wear me out and possibly undo all the progress I'd made, but also because it could potentially harm my children. And that would be the worst possible thing I could ever have to bear.

I went home and immediately began to meditate. Through meditation and soul retrieval (a process of deep inward reflection), I was able to put back the pieces of my heart and soul that had been damaged from feeling such harsh judgments. It felt like the deepest parts of me had actually fallen to pieces. I had to inwardly pick up each one and gently replace it so I could feel whole again. I told my inner self that it was okay; that all would be well, because I was strong and brave—and because I knew the truth about me, as well as the truth about all my actions and thoughts and feelings, and I owned all of it. People can, and will, think what they want to, but that does not mean that they know another person's truth—mine or anyone else's. No one can really know the truth of another person. To really know another person takes tremendous courage, strength, and love—not just for the other person, but for oneself. Most of what we think we know is judgment, not knowledge . . . and certainly not wisdom.

None of this changed the facts. I owned who I was and what I did, but I was not going to cave in because of other people's judgments. I have to live with the truth of who I am and of all my actions, thoughts, and feelings—just as everyone else does. How I do that and how I feel about it is between me and the Great Spirit, not between me and anyone else. It is simply not anyone else's business.

But back to the facts: I did not lose custody of the children, as a lot of people might assume would be the case for a parent who has, or has had, an affinity for hard drugs. My ex and I have joint custody, but the children live with him full-time. This was a mutually reached nontraditional choice that he and I made for the sake of the children. After rehab, I was not in a good place, physically or emotionally, even though I was making solid progress and growing stronger every day. Our decision was that it made more sense for the kids to stay in their home, with nanny care and financial stability. If they would have come to live with me at that time, it would have meant all three of us cramped in a small apartment, with uncertain financial stability—and for the kids, it also would have meant living full-time with a mother who was exhausted from attempting to get through all this on her own.

When my ex and I made the choice, I felt sure it was the right one for the kids and for me—and I still think that. The flash of insight that caused me to feel others' harsh judgments did make me feel embarrassed and ashamed and hurt. Because judgments are inflicted, whether intentionally or not, they create wounds, which, if we do not heal them, leave scars. Meditation made me realize that I could not allow my wounds to remain unhealed, because I was not willing to be scarred by people's judgments. Remember, people will always think something—or feel it or say it or act on it—but that doesn't have to change the way we think about ourselves. We, not they, know the truth. You can only stand tall and walk proud when you know the truth—and when you own it. There is no alternative. You cannot walk around the path to the truth; you have to follow the way *through* to find it and to own it—and then you will never again feel lost or alone.

After that meditation and soul retrieval, my self-confidence and courage were stronger than ever. I was able to face people without fear for two reasons: First, I don't really care what people think of me, and they're going to judge me whether I care or not; second, and even more important, I have received unconditional love, forgiveness, and acceptance from the only person who matters—me. I have given myself the inner strength and support to know that, no matter what, the kids and I are going to be fine. I am guided, loved, and supported at every step of this journey called life. By loving myself unconditionally, I am assured that I shall never really be abandoned or feel alone—because I will never abandon myself again . . . and because the Great Spirit loves and protects us all.

It is also true that I have no idea where the journey will ultimately end—no one does. (I also do not know what might be in store for me as a result of my having signed legal papers without sufficient legal advice.) But again, I do know that the children and I will be stronger and healthier—and in a better spiritual place, with a deep and abiding sense of unconditional support, security, and love. I know this because I know that the Great Spirit will never abandon us—no matter how bad and shameful I think I've made things.

An enormous tidal wave had just crashed upon me and awakened me from a long, slow slumber. Yes, this was exactly what I intended to explore; and yes, I would listen only to myself for the answers. My growing interest in metaphysics did not mean I had to abandon my other passions or that which I identified as what made me, *me*. I could still rock in stilettos and tight jeans, *and* be in touch with the universe, all at the same time. I would reach out to others going through this same situation, because I wanted to let them know that yes, it is really happening; and no, it doesn't mean they have to give up the rest of who they are. Our true self is a combination of the deepest part of us (higher self) and the part of us that we take out into the world every day. In other words, our true self is the whole of us.

This might seem complicated, even overwhelming. But, really, being our true self just means sticking to one simple principle: Stand tall, walk proud, and own it.

> *A hero is no braver than an ordinary man, but he is braver five minutes longer.*
> **—Ralph Waldo Emerson**

Don't Drink the "Hater-ade"

Hope, trust, faith, and love. Life is not worth much without these things, no matter what material possessions or achievements one might garner.

Hope, trust, faith, and love. These are the things that matter, and they are also the things that last. The *only* things that matter and last.

I have heard many an addict say that addiction/recovery was the best thing that could have happened to him or her. I never understood how losing everything could be a good thing—until it happened to me. It forced me to evaluate my inner self, my definition of gratitude, and my personal struggle to balance my strengths and weaknesses. I am finally comfortable saying that I feel really good in my own skin. An unconventional and painful journey has allowed me to fully become my true self, for which I am grateful to a depth that is beyond expression in words.

Choices and experiences are all part of life. I've described life as a journey, but it's also a game of sorts. When we view it as a game, it's easy to see that there are two kinds of players: those who love the game, and those who hate it. I realize that the world is filled with unhappy people who refuse to enjoy playing the game—that is, living—because of fear. At the same time, there are people who have made successful plays by throwing all caution to the wind.

There will always be "haters" who try to knock us down, because seeing others really live in happiness only heightens their own fear. Misery loves company, as the saying goes. At the end of the day, we each have to decide whether we're going to love or hate life—regardless of the hand we're dealt. In other words, it's more enjoyable to drink lemonade than to suck on a lemon. I stepped out of line big time, and I own that—but I refuse to stand in an endless lineup to drink "hater-ade." Life is just too short and too precious to do that!

So, instead, I listen to and follow my voice—only mine, not anyone else's. I practice following hope, faith, trust, love, and acceptance—each and every day, and I believe that these will continue to lead me along a path of endless possibilities and great joy.

Although it is occasionally hard to follow my own advice, I am certain that I am making healthy choices. The only thing I am addicted to now is a good thing—*hope.*

I happily absorb that hope, and I am utterly captivated by the simplicity of it. For me, hope is the radiant light of the universe, the power of the Great Spirit that shines eternally. Hope's simplicity stems from this intense strength and power lying behind it; because of this, hope can never, ever be taken away from me—or you, or anyone.

The future will always remain a great mystery—for me and for us all. But I have high hopes that much good lies ahead. Right now I have hope that I can show my children I'm okay: I am solidly taking care of myself so that they will see I am worth believing in. By believing in me, they will grow up strong and believe in themselves.

Most of all, I pray that we all can see how necessary it is to never lose sight of hope, trust, faith, and love—either within ourselves or among one another.

May you have warmth in your igloo, oil in your lamp, and peace in your heart.

—Eskimo Proverb

Afterword

I wrote this book as a conscious choice to share my journey with others. I did this with the intention of instilling a sense of freedom, empowerment, support, encouragement, and, above all, hope in everyone who reads this book. It is my heartfelt wish that this book also brings comfort and healing to all those who read it.

Society propagates the idea that addiction is embarrassing and shameful. But I am here to tell you that addiction does not have to be embarrassing or shameful—and, more important, that true recovery can lead to grace, strength, courage, and peace. Yes, these are personal struggles; but the more we accept one another's weaknesses and shortcomings, instead of passing judgment, the easier it becomes to heal ourselves and find strength within shameful and embarrassing moments—as these relate not just to addiction, but also to life in general. Embarrassment and shame have deep roots—a long-ago moment can resonate through a lifetime, creating an endless cycle of pain. Acknowledging such moments and letting them out into the light of day is the only way to move beyond them—to live in freedom and peace. We have all been there, addicts and nonaddicts alike; this is why I feel that a lot of people can, and will, relate to my story.

The right message at the right time can be life-changing. Spirituality was my message. It came through when I realized that it is not a religion; it is a process. I stand tall, walk proud, and own who I am—and, yes, I do it in tight jeans and stilettos—and I do it because all of that is who I am. Not everyone has traveled a similar path to mine. Some who have will find that my experiences and solutions resonate for them; others might not. I encourage all of them to find their own path and their own solutions, but most of all, to be true to themselves and to nourish themselves tenderly and consistently—body, mind, heart, and soul. And to give each and every person they meet the space to do the same, without judgment and without reservation.

We each and all are humble travelers on the same road: life. We each do the best we can. Perhaps the most we can do for one another is to remember this:

Be kind, for everyone you meet is fighting a hard battle.
—Philo of Alexandria

About the Author

Brienne Joelle enjoys painting, mixed-media collage and soap making as her forms of artistic expression. She also delights in reading, writing, and soaking up all that nature has to offer. The Pacific Northwest is where she can be found pursuing these joys. Her twins, her pug dog, and her love of life all strengthen her connection to the strong creative force of the universe.

She invites you to visit her website, www.violet-crow.com, to discover her handmade, all natural, small batches of goat's milk bath products. She discovered a hands-on hobby that not only connects her to nature but gives back to the community, as well. Enjoy and be inspired by her beautiful, all natural products.

Works Cited

Adam. *The Path of the Dream Healer: My Journey Through the Miraculous World of Energy Healing.* New York: Penguin Group, 2006. Print.

Dillard, Sherrie. *Discover Your Psychic Type: Developing and Using Your Natural Intuition.* Woodbury, Minnesota: Llewellyn Publications, 2008. Print.

Newton, Michael, PhD. *Journey of Souls: Case Studies of Life Between Lives.* Woodbury, Minnesota: Llewellyn Publications, 1994. Print.

Osho. *Creativity: Unleashing the Forces Within.* New York, New York: St. Martin's Press, 1999. Print.

Virtue, Doreen, PhD. *The Lightworker's Way: Awakening Your Spiritual Power to Know and Heal.* Carlsbad, California: Hay House, Inc., 1997. Print.

Williamson, Marianne. *A Woman's Worth.* New York: Random House Publishing Group, 1994. Print.